I0517741

REIKI AND THE FIVE ELEMENTS:

BALANCING ENERGY THROUGH NATURE'S WISDOM

REIKI WISDOM SERIES
Beyond the Symbols — The Path to True Mastery

Sacred Symbol of Reiki Wisdom

The sacred combination of the **circle, triangle, intersecting lines**, and **pentagram** represents the harmonious flow of spiritual and physical energy.

- The **circle** symbolizes **wholeness** and **spiritual protection**, reflecting the infinite and interconnected nature of Reiki energy.
- The **triangle** embodies **creation** and **balance**, representing the three pillars of Reiki — **mind, body, and spirit** — working in harmony.
- The **three converging lines** reflect **unity** and **focused intent**, directing energy flow through the chakras and meridians.
- The **pentagram** signifies **mastery of the elements** (earth, fire, water, air, and spirit) and the awakening of spiritual wisdom.

This symbol represents the manifestation of divine energy into physical reality through balance, alignment, and focused intention. It reflects the path to enlightenment — where mind, body, and spirit align to unlock deep healing and spiritual mastery.

Grand Master, Constance Santego

REIKI AND THE FIVE ELEMENTS

VOL. III OF THE REIKI WISDOM SERIES

Beyond the Symbols — The Path to True Mastery

Dr. Constance Santego

Maximillian Enterprises
Kelowna, BC

REIKI AND THE FIVE ELEMENTS
Copyright ° 2025 by Dr. Constance Santego.

Copy Editor and Interior Design: Constance Santego
Book Layout: °2017 BookDesignTemplates.com
Cover Design: Jennifer Louie

Ordering Information:
Quantity sales. Special discounts are available on quantity purchases by corporations, associations, and others. For details, contact the address below.

Trade paperback ISBN: 978-1-990062-65-0

eBook ISBN: 978-1-990062-66-7

Created and published In Canada. Printed and bound in the United States of America

First Edition
Published by Maximillian Enterprises
Kelowna, BC Canada
www.constancesantego.ca

Dedication

To all Reiki instructors, practitioners, and healers — from beginners to masters — who dedicate themselves to the art of healing through energy. May this work deepen your connection to the universal flow and empower you to unlock greater wisdom, balance, and healing.

"Through wisdom and intention, your hands become a channel for healing and transformation."
—Dr. Constance Santego

ALSO BY DR. CONSTANCE SANTEGO

NOVELS

Illegitimate Grace

Okanagan Trilogy:

Beneath the Vineyards
Under the Okanagan Sun
Guardian of the Lake

The Nine Spiritual Gifts Series:
Journey of a Soul – (Vol 1 Michael)
Language of a Soul – (Vol 2 Gabriel)
Prophecy of a Soul – (Vol 3 Bath Kol)
Healing of a Soul – (Vol 4 Raphael)
Miracles of a Soul – (Vol 5 Hamied)
Knowledge of a Soul – (Vol 6 Raziel)
Wisdom of a Soul – (Vol 7 Uriel)
Faith of a Soul – (Vol 8 Pistis Sophia)

NONFICTION
The Intuitive Life, The Gift Of Prophecy, Third Edition
Fairy Tales, Dreams And Reality… Where Are You On Your
Path? Second Edition
Your Persona… The Mask You Wear
Archangel Michael's Soul Retrieval Guide
Tesla And The Future Of Energy Medicine
Beyond Tesla: *Advancing The Science Of Energy Healing*
Tesla's Code: *Mastering Energy, Frequency, And Creative Power*
Scaling Beyond 6 Figures: *Strategies for Health & Wellness Professionals*
Beyond the Mind: *Harnessing the Power of Astral Projection*

for Creative Awakening
Bend, Don't Break: *Finding Your Way Back to Abundance*
Ring Therapy: *A Guide to Healing and Balance*
Ring Therapy Pocket Guide
Floraopathy™: *The Art and Science of Vibrational Healing with Essential Oils*

REIKI WISDOM, SERIES:

Angelic Lifestyle, a Vibrant Lifestyle
Angelic Lifestyle 42-Day Energy Cleanse
Reiki and the Power of The Joint Points: *Unlocking Energy Pathways for Healing* (Vol I)
Reiki and Karmic Healing: *Releasing Patterens From Past Lives* (Vol II)
Reiki and the Five Elements (Vol III)

SECRETS OF A HEALER, SERIES:
Magic Of Aromatherapy (Vol I)
Magic Of Reflexology (Vol II)
Magic Of The Gifts (Vol III)
Magic Of Muscle Testing (Vol IV)
Magic Of Iridology (Vol V)
Magic Of Massage (Vol VI)
Magic Of Hypnotherapy (Vol VII)
Magic Of Reiki (Vol VIII)
Magic Of Advanced Aromatherapy (Vol IX)
Magic Of Esthetics (Vol X)
The Reiki Master's Manual (Vol XI)

ADULT COLORING JOURNALS

SERIES-ZEN COLORING:
Quantum Energy and Mindful Living Journal (Vol 1)
Reiki Energy Journal (Vol 2)
Nine Spiritual Gifts Journal (Vol 3)
I Forgive Journal (Vol 4)

FOR CHILDREN
I am Big Tonight. I Don't Need the Light

Contents

Preface

Reiki Wisdom: Unlocking Energy Pathways for Healing

Reiki and the Five Elements
Balancing Energy Through Nature's Wisdom

Reiki has been at the heart of my healing practice since 1999, guiding not just my personal journey, but also the thousands of students I've taught over the years. It has always been about more than hand positions or technique—Reiki is about restoring the natural flow of energy, connecting with the unseen rhythms of life, and learning to trust in something greater than ourselves.

In all my years of practice, I've witnessed how energy becomes blocked not just by physical tension or emotional trauma, but also by being out of sync with the natural world. That insight led me to explore the ancient wisdom of the Five Elements—Water, Wood, Fire, Earth, and Metal—as a framework to understand how our energy, emotions, and physical health are deeply intertwined with nature's cycles.

This book is the result of that exploration—a fusion of Reiki energy healing with the timeless principles of Five Element Theory from Traditional Chinese Medicine. It offers a new way to approach Reiki sessions, one that honors the elemental forces within us and all around us. By tuning into seasonal shifts, emotional patterns, and elemental imbalances, we can use Reiki to bring ourselves back into harmony—mind, body, and spirit.

Whether you're a seasoned Reiki Master or just beginning your journey, my hope is that *Reiki and the Five Elements* will expand your perspective and deepen your practice. Through its pages, may you come to see not only your clients and students more clearly, but also yourself—as part of a vast, living system where healing flows as naturally as the changing of the seasons.

With nature's wisdom and Reiki's light,
Dr. Constance Santego
Grand Reiki Master

Note to Reader

Reiki is a powerful complementary therapy, but it is not intended to replace conventional medical care. If you are experiencing physical, emotional, mental, or spiritual challenges, you should always consult with a qualified healthcare provider or mental health professional.

Think of it this way—if you break a bone, you'll need a doctor, nurses, and the medical team at the hospital to reset and support your physical healing. Reiki, however, can play a supportive role in managing pain, reducing stress, and encouraging emotional balance throughout your recovery.

Integrative Medicine emphasizes your active role in your own health. What you eat, how you move, the level of stress you carry, the thoughts you entertain, and the energy you allow into your life all have a direct impact on your well-being. This book builds on that philosophy—adding nature's wisdom through the Five Elements to help you better understand your internal landscape and how to work with it, not against it.

Reiki is an effective tool for stress relief, clearing energetic blockages, improving awareness, and aligning with your body's natural rhythms. When combined with the elemental forces of Water, Wood, Fire, Earth, and Metal, it becomes even more powerful as a tool for reflection, balance, and transformation.

As a reminder:

- A valid Reiki Level II certificate (signed by a certified Reiki Master) is required if you plan to **charge money for treating others**.
- A Reiki Level III (Master/Teacher) certificate is required if you wish to **teach and attune others** to Reiki.

You are always in charge of your own healing. Reiki is here to support you—but the energy responds best when you show up for yourself with intention, consistency, and a willingness to grow.

Let nature guide you, and let Reiki lead the way.

Learning Outcome

Reiki and the Five Elements: Balancing Energy Through Nature's Wisdom

This book is a transformative guide that brings together two ancient systems of healing: Reiki and the Five Element Theory from Traditional Chinese Medicine. It provides a comprehensive understanding of how the elements—Water, Wood, Fire, Earth, and Metal—interact with our energy, emotions, and physical well-being. By learning to identify elemental imbalances and work with them through Reiki, you'll discover how to support healing on a deeper, more holistic level.

Whether you are new to Reiki or an experienced practitioner, this book offers new insights, tools, and approaches to enhance your personal healing journey and professional practice.

By the end of this book, you will have a thorough understanding of the following:

Part 1: Foundations of Elemental Energy

- The origin and philosophy of the Five Element Theory and how it complements Reiki.
- How each element relates to specific emotions, organs, seasons, and energetic patterns.

- The relationship between the Five Elements and the chakra system.
- How imbalances in elemental energy manifest physically, emotionally, and spiritually.

Part 2: Reiki Techniques for Elemental Balancing

- How to assess which element(s) are in excess or deficiency in yourself or clients.
- How to tailor Reiki sessions to support elemental healing.
- Reiki hand positions, breathwork, and visualizations for each element.
- Using affirmations, color therapy, essential oils, and crystals aligned with each element.

Part 3: Integrating Elemental Wisdom into Your Practice

- Creating seasonal healing rituals using Reiki and the Five Elements.
- Aligning your energy healing sessions with natural cycles—solstices, equinoxes, and lunar phases.
- How to build Elemental Reiki sessions for clients based on emotional or energetic needs.
- Practical tools for combining Reiki with Five Element principles in a clinical or wellness setting.

Part 4: Self-Healing, Reflection, and Spiritual Growth

- Journaling prompts and meditations to explore your elemental strengths and imbalances.
- Tools for deepening your relationship with nature's rhythms and inner healing.

- How to use elemental insight for personal development and intuitive guidance.
- Exercises for reconnecting with your body, your environment, and the universal energy that flows through all things.

This book will serve as both a practical guide and a spiritual companion, helping you explore your healing gifts in a new light. You will learn how to harmonize the flow of Reiki energy through the lens of nature's wisdom, empowering you to create powerful, personalized healing experiences—for yourself and those you serve.

Whether you are beginning your Reiki journey or expanding your path, *Reiki and the Five Elements* will enrich your practice and deepen your understanding of the energy that connects us all.

"Reiki Wisdom is not just the flow of energy—it is the remembrance of who you truly are, the healing of what you no longer need, and the awakening of all that you are meant to become."

— Dr. Constance Santego

Introduction – Reconnecting with Nature's Energy Through Reiki

In traditional Reiki training, practitioners are taught to focus on the chakra system and the flow of universal life force energy to promote healing. While this foundation remains essential, there is another layer of wisdom often left untapped—the energy of the natural world, reflected in the ancient system known as the Five Elements.

The Five Elements—**Water, Wood, Fire, Earth, and Metal**—are more than philosophical ideas. They are dynamic energies that shape the rhythms of nature and the energetic blueprint of our bodies, minds, and spirits. Each element is associated with specific organs, emotions, seasons, colors, and physical patterns. When one or more of these elements becomes imbalanced, it can disrupt not only our physical health but also our emotional stability and spiritual clarity.

This book explores how **Reiki energy can be aligned with the Five Elements** to deepen your healing practice, enhance self-awareness, and restore balance on a holistic level. By working with both systems together, we can tune into the natural cycles of life—just as the Earth transitions from season to season, so do we. When we bring this understanding into our Reiki sessions, the results can be profound.

Reiki naturally supports the free flow of energy. When paired with elemental wisdom, it becomes an even more refined tool—one that can **target emotional imbalances, align seasonal patterns**, and **awaken a deeper connection to the world around and within us**. For example:

- A Water imbalance may present as fear, fatigue, or lower back pain. Reiki can calm and replenish this energy.
- A Fire imbalance may show up as restlessness, anxiety, or insomnia. Reiki can soothe and stabilize.
- An Earth imbalance might lead to overthinking or digestive issues. Reiki can ground and restore.

As practitioners, we are also stewards of nature's rhythm. Understanding how to read the body through the lens of the Five Elements allows us to offer Reiki not just as a healing tool—but as a **bridge between humanity and the Earth's natural intelligence**.

In the chapters that follow, you'll be introduced to the energy and qualities of each element, how they correspond to the chakra system, and how to work with them using Reiki hand positions, visualizations, affirmations, crystals, essential oils, and seasonal rituals. You'll also learn how to assess elemental imbalances in yourself and others, and how to design Reiki sessions that align with nature's cycles.

Whether you are new to Reiki or a seasoned practitioner, this book invites you to step into a **deeper, more intuitive**

relationship with your healing gifts. May it awaken in you a renewed sense of balance, connection, and elemental wisdom.

Let us return to nature. Let us return to energy. Let us return to ourselves.

Dr. Constance Santego
Grand Reiki Master

PART 1:
THE FOUNDATION

Chapter 1: What is Reiki?

Remembering the Energy Within

If you've already journeyed through the pages of *Reiki and the Power of the Joint Points*, then you've begun to sense that Reiki is more than just a healing technique. It's a relationship—a quiet, powerful language between you and the unseen forces that guide, nourish, and restore balance.

But let's take a step back. Not to the basics you've already learned, but to the roots of where this all began—not just historically, but energetically.

The word **Reiki** is often translated as "universal life force energy." It sounds simple, almost poetic, and yet it carries the weight of millennia. While the modern system of Reiki was formalized by **Mikao Usui** in early 20th-century Japan, the essence of Reiki—the transmission of healing through the hands and heart—has existed in some form throughout all cultures and times. From the laying on of hands in ancient spiritual traditions to the subtle energy work of Eastern

Conscious breathwork and focused mantras help direct and amplify the flow of energy, promote balance and emotional release.

medicine, the core truth remains: **we are energetic beings, and we are meant to flow**.

Mikao Usui's teachings were not just a method—they were a lifestyle. Reiki was not designed to be dissected or standardized, but to be **experienced**. Usui himself taught that Reiki is a path of personal development. Yes, it heals. But more importantly, it awakens. When you place your hands on yourself or another and allow the energy to move, you are remembering something ancient and instinctual—something the body has always known.

Reiki is about **connection**.
Connection to your body.
Connection to your breath.
Connection to Spirit, Source, or the universal pulse that beats beneath all life.

In *The Power of the Joint Points*, you learned that energy gathers, pauses, and often stagnates at the hinges of our physical body. You explored how these "crossroads" hold emotional and spiritual imprints—and how Reiki can release them.

In this book, we expand the lens. Rather than looking at the body as isolated energy centers, we now look at the **ecosystem of energy** that lives both within and around us. Where joints were the gates, **elements are the terrain**. Earth. Water. Fire. Wood. Metal. Each one carries its own rhythm, emotion, and energetic lesson. And when balanced, they guide us toward a more harmonious, grounded life.

So if you ask, "What is Reiki?"—it is still what it has always been. A gentle, intelligent force. A light in your hands. A bridge between healing and becoming. But now, we move beyond technique and begin to **walk with the elements**, understanding how Reiki can dance with nature's wisdom to bring you deeper into balance.

This is Reiki, not as something you do, but as something you **live**.

Conscious breathwork and focused mantras help direct and amplify the flow of energy, promoti *balance and emotional release.*

Life Force Energy and the Auric Field

The Space Between You and the World

You may have felt it before—the subtle shift in the air when someone walks into a room. Or the heaviness that clings to your body after a difficult conversation. Or perhaps the radiant sense of peace that settles in when you're alone in nature, surrounded by trees, water, or wind. These sensations don't arise from your skin or muscles—they come from something more expansive, something just beyond your physical edges.

This is the **auric field**.
And it's very much alive.

The auric field, also known as the **human energy field**, is the invisible yet tangible field of energy that surrounds and interpenetrates your body. It's layered, dynamic, and constantly responding to your inner world—your thoughts, emotions, intentions—and to the outer world—your environment, relationships, and experiences.

In Reiki, we refer to this vital energy as **Ki** (in Japanese), or **Chi** (in Chinese), **Prana** (in Sanskrit), and even **Ruach** in Hebrew teachings. This **life force energy** is the foundation of all existence, flowing through everything and connecting us to the pulse of creation. It animates your body, nourishes your cells, and bridges your physical being with your spiritual essence.

When your auric field is balanced and strong, you feel clear, confident, and grounded. Energy flows smoothly through your chakras and meridians. Your emotions feel manageable, your intuition is sharp, and your physical body thrives.

But when your auric field becomes **distorted, drained, or overwhelmed**, things begin to unravel. You may feel tired, emotionally reactive, forgetful, irritable, or disconnected. You may even start absorbing energy that doesn't belong to you—taking on the emotions, fears, or fatigue of others, often without realizing it.

This is where Reiki becomes a powerful ally.

Reiki works beyond the skin. When your hands channel Reiki energy, it flows not only through the physical body but also through the **auric layers**—cleansing, harmonizing, and restoring your energetic boundaries. It helps remove the fog, realign the vibration, and bring you back to a natural, healthy rhythm.

The Five Elements, too, influence this field. Think of each element as a current or frequency flowing through the auric space:

- **Water** brings depth, calm, and introspection to the field.
- **Wood** stirs movement, growth, and drive.
- **Fire** ignites joy, passion, and warmth.
- **Earth** stabilizes, nurtures, and grounds.
- **Metal** sharpens clarity, order, and the ability to release.

Conscious breathwork and focused mantras help direct and amplify the flow of energy, promot
balance and emotional release.

If your auric field is like a garden, the Five Elements are the seasons that nurture its growth. And Reiki? Reiki is the **sunlight** that warms it and the **rain** that clears the dust away.

In this chapter, you'll explore how to sense, work with, and protect your auric field using Reiki and elemental awareness. You'll learn techniques for energetic hygiene, grounding your field, and identifying when an element may be creating discord in your energy body.

Your auric field is not just a container—it's your **first line of communication with the world**. By keeping it balanced, nourished, and flowing, you create a space where healing is not only possible—it becomes inevitable.

Reiki Levels and Attunements

The Sacred Spiral of Awakening

Reiki is not simply a skill to be acquired—it is a journey of initiation. And like any sacred path, it unfolds in stages, each one revealing deeper layers of wisdom, energy, and self-awareness. These stages are known as the **Reiki levels**, and each one is marked by a profound energetic shift called an **attunement**.

If you've already experienced a Reiki attunement, then you know—it is unlike anything else.

It's not a technique taught with words, but a **transmission**, passed from teacher to student, spirit to soul. During an attunement, a Reiki Master opens your energy channels and aligns you with the universal life force in a more direct, conscious way. It is both a **remembering** and a **reawakening**—like tuning a dusty radio dial to the clear frequency of Source.

Reiki Level I: The Awakening – Earth Energy

The first level is often described as the physical or "hands-on" level. But beneath the surface, something much deeper is happening. Reiki I reconnects you to the Earth. It stabilizes your energy body, grounds your awareness, and awakens your hands as instruments of healing.

This level corresponds beautifully with the **Earth element**—solid, foundational, nurturing. After your first attunement,

Conscious breathwork and focused mantras help direct and amplify the flow of energy, promote balance and emotional release.

you may notice subtle shifts: a heightened sensitivity in your palms, a calming presence in your body, or emotional releases you didn't expect. This is your system learning to flow.

Reiki Level II: The Expansion – Water and Fire Energy

Reiki II opens the gateway to working beyond space and time. With this attunement, you're introduced to the sacred symbols, and your practice deepens—no longer limited by touch or proximity. You begin to feel energy moving through you like a current.

This level carries the dual forces of **Water and Fire**. Water for its intuitive, emotional wisdom—the ability to feel into another's energy from across the room or across the world. And Fire for its clarity and transformation—the burning away of old beliefs as you step into your power.

Distance healing becomes possible. Mental and emotional healing becomes tangible. The work becomes more refined.

Reiki Level III (Master) and Level IV (Teacher): The Embodiment – Metal and Wood Energy

The Master level is a spiritual threshold. Here, you're not just practicing Reiki—you're becoming it.

Metal energy brings **refinement, precision, and integrity**, helping you discern truth from illusion. Wood brings the **vision and courage** to grow beyond your old limitations. As a Master, you become both healer and student—always evolving, always listening.

And if you choose to teach, to pass on attunements yourself, you become a **guardian of the lineage**, a living link in a chain of light stretching back to Usui and beyond. You learn not just to activate others—but to hold space for their unfolding.

An attunement is not just an energetic upgrade—it is a **sacred agreement**. One that says:
"I am ready to remember who I am."
"I am willing to be a vessel for light."
"I am open to healing—not only others, but myself."

As we explore the Five Elements in the chapters to come, remember that each Reiki level brings you closer to them— because the more you awaken your inner healer, the more aligned you become with the natural forces of the universe.

The attunement is not the destination. It's the **doorway**. And now, we walk through it—into the elemental heart of Reiki.

Conscious breathwork and focused mantras help direct and amplify the flow of energy, promoting balance and emotional release.

The Chakra System & Reiki Hand Positions

Touching the Energy Within

If life force energy is the river that flows through us, the **chakras** are the stepping stones that help us cross it—centers of energy where the physical, emotional, mental, and spiritual bodies converge.

You may already be familiar with the traditional seven chakra system:
Root, Sacral, Solar Plexus, Heart, Throat, Third Eye, and Crown.
Each one resonates with a different frequency, governs different organs and emotions, and holds lessons we must walk through again and again on our journey toward wholeness.

But chakras are not fixed or mechanical—they're **fluid and responsive**, shifting with your experiences, beliefs, and the energy you carry. One moment they may radiate freely, the next they may contract or distort due to stress, fear, or emotional suppression.

This is where **Reiki hand positions** become a form of sacred conversation—each placement an invitation to listen, release, and realign.

The Hands as Channels of Wisdom

In Reiki, the hands are not just tools—they are **transmitters**, **receivers**, and **sensors**. They allow us to feel energy, direct it, and intuit where healing is needed. Every hand position in Reiki has a purpose, not only physically, but energetically.

When you place your hands on the heart chakra, you are not just offering comfort—you are amplifying compassion, inviting grief to surface, and allowing love to return. When your hands rest over the root chakra, you're not just grounding energy—you are speaking safety into the body.

Each hand position aligns with a chakra, and each chakra can be influenced by one or more of the Five Elements. As you practice, you'll begin to see how elemental imbalances show up in chakra patterns:

- A blocked **Throat Chakra** may reflect a **Metal** imbalance—difficulty letting go, or unspoken grief.
- A depleted **Solar Plexus** may reveal an exhausted **Wood** energy—stalled creativity or suppressed anger.
- An overactive **Crown Chakra** could indicate too much **Fire**—burnout or spiritual disconnection.

By placing your hands on these centers with intention, you don't force energy—you **invite flow**. Reiki knows where to go. Your job is to **listen**, allow, and hold space.

Conscious breathwork and focused mantras help direct and amplify the flow of energy, promote balance and emotional release.

Chakras & Their Elemental Echoes

Let's briefly align the chakras with their elemental energies, which you'll explore in depth in later chapters:

- **Root Chakra (Earth + Water)** – Survival, safety, physical foundation
- **Sacral Chakra (Water)** – Creativity, emotion, sensuality
- **Solar Plexus (Wood + Fire)** – Confidence, direction, willpower
- **Heart Chakra (Fire + Air)** – Love, compassion, harmony
- **Throat Chakra (Metal)** – Expression, truth, communication
- **Third Eye Chakra (Wood + Ether)** – Intuition, perception, inner vision
- **Crown Chakra (Metal + Ether)** – Spiritual connection, divine awareness

As you work with Reiki and the Five Elements together, you'll begin to feel the **interconnectedness**—how the energy of nature flows through each chakra, and how your hand placements become like tuning forks, calling each center back into resonance.

A Living Practice

Reiki hand positions are not rigid formulas. They are starting points—anchors that help the practitioner and the receiver feel safe, open, and supported.

Sometimes, your intuition will guide your hands to hover instead of touch. Other times, you'll be led to stay longer at one center, even if the session has "moved on." Trust the energy. Trust your body. Trust that Reiki flows where it's needed most.

Remember, you are not the healer—**you are the bridge**. Your hands simply remind the body how to heal itself.

In the next chapters, we'll begin to layer the elemental framework onto your Reiki practice. You'll learn how to identify imbalances through both chakras and elements, and how to craft sessions that are responsive to the energy of the moment, the season, and the soul.

But for now—pause. Place your hands on your heart. Take a breath.
Feel that warmth? That's Reiki.
That's you.

Conscious breathwork and focused mantras help direct and amplify the flow of energy, promot balance and emotional release.

*NOTE: If you're curious to experience energy in action, I invite you to watch a simple yet powerful **proof-of-energy experiment** I recorded on my YouTube channel. It's a visual demonstration of how life force energy interacts with the space around us—something many people don't believe until they feel or see it for themselves.

You can find the video here:
https://youtu.be/jnZAOGYWy2M

Let it serve as a reminder: **energy is real**—even when unseen. And with Reiki, you're learning how to work with it consciously, with purpose and intention.

Chapter 2: The Wisdom of the Five Elements

Origin in Traditional Chinese Medicine

Before there were microscopes, lab tests, or even stethoscopes, there was observation—of the sky, the body, the seasons, and the natural rhythms of life. Ancient healers saw that everything in nature moved in cycles. Trees blossomed, rivers flowed, fire transformed, metal forged structure, and earth gave birth to it all.

From these patterns emerged one of the most elegant and time-tested philosophies of healing: the **Five Element Theory**, or **Wu Xing**, as it is known in Traditional Chinese Medicine (TCM).

The Five Elements—**Wood, Fire, Earth, Metal, and Water**— are not literal substances, but rather dynamic expressions of energy. They represent processes, archetypes, emotional patterns, and physical systems, both in the world around us and within the body. The Five Elements are the language of harmony and transformation. They show us how energy moves, interacts, changes, and renews.

Each element is associated with a **season, emotion, organ system, color**, and even **personality traits**. Together, they

Conscious breathwork and focused mantras help direct and amplify the flow of energy, promoti[ng] balance and emotional release.

form an intricate energetic map of human nature and the natural world. This system doesn't just explain how we get sick—it teaches us how to stay balanced.

Let's take a brief look at the Five Elements through the lens of their origins:

Wood is the energy of spring, growth, and direction.

It governs the **liver and gallbladder**, holds the emotion of **anger**, and reflects our ability to plan, decide, and take action. Wood is like a sprouting seed, bursting through soil, reaching toward light. Too much Wood energy and we become rigid or easily frustrated. Too little, and we feel lost, unmotivated, or indecisive.

Fire is the spark of summer, passion, joy, and connection.

It governs the **heart and small intestine** and is tied to **love, laughter**, and intimacy. Fire gives us warmth, charisma, and the courage to express ourselves. An imbalance may show up as anxiety, burnout, or emotional volatility—or its opposite, emotional numbness.

Earth is the transition between seasons—a place of nurturing, stability, and digestion.

It rules the **spleen and stomach**, and carries the emotion of **worry** or overthinking. When in balance, Earth grounds us, nourishes our body, and provides emotional security. Out of balance, we may feel scattered, clingy, or unable to digest our experiences—physically or mentally.

Metal is the crispness of autumn, the energy of refinement, boundaries, and letting go.

It governs the **lungs and large intestine**, and carries the emotion of **grief**. Metal helps us see what no longer serves us and release it with grace. It gives structure and dignity. When imbalanced, we may struggle with sadness, perfectionism, or detachment.

Water is the stillness of winter, the essence of rest, restoration, and introspection.

It rules the **kidneys and bladder**, and holds the emotion of **fear**. Water teaches us to conserve energy, trust the unknown, and access deep inner wisdom. Too much Water energy may feel overwhelming or fearful; too little leaves us depleted and disconnected.

The brilliance of the Five Element system lies in its **constant movement**. These energies are never static—they feed one another in a **creative cycle** (Water nourishes Wood, Wood fuels Fire…), and keep each other in check through a **controlling cycle** (Fire melts Metal, Metal cuts Wood…).

By understanding these natural rhythms, we begin to see our own imbalances with compassion, not judgment. We stop asking, "What's wrong with me?" and begin asking, "What is out of balance?" That subtle shift changes everything.

And this is where Reiki comes in.

Reiki gives us the **tool to restore balance**. When you align your Reiki practice with the wisdom of the Five Elements,

Conscious breathwork and focused mantras help direct and amplify the flow of energy, promot balance and emotional release.

you begin to tailor your sessions intuitively—listening not only to what the body says, but to what nature is whispering as well.

The Five Elements in Harmony

Overview of Wood, Fire, Earth, Metal, and Water

The Five Elements are not isolated parts of a system—they are a **symphony of energies**, constantly moving, shifting, and flowing through all of life. In Traditional Chinese Medicine and Taoist philosophy, these elements represent the phases of transformation, the emotional currents that shape us, and the energetic forces that guide our growth, rest, action, and renewal.

As Reiki practitioners, when we understand the **personality and purpose** of each element, we gain a powerful map for reading energy—not just in our clients, but in ourselves. Below is an overview of each element, described not only by its physical correspondences but also by its deeper emotional and energetic qualities.

Wood – The Force of Growth and Direction

- **Season:** Spring
- **Organs:** Liver & Gallbladder
- **Chakra Influence:** Solar Plexus (willpower), Third Eye (vision)
- **Emotion:** Anger (when blocked), assertiveness (when balanced)
- **Elemental Wisdom:** Wood is the pioneer. It pushes forward, stretches toward the light, and insists on growth. It helps us envision, plan, and act. When Wood is balanced, we feel driven, focused, and adaptable. When imbalanced, we may feel stuck,

Conscious breathwork and focused mantras help direct and amplify the flow of energy, promote balance and emotional release.

indecisive, or quick to anger. Reiki harmonizes Wood energy by soothing frustration, supporting clarity, and restoring emotional flow.

Fire – The Flame of Passion and Connection

- **Season:** Summer
- **Organs:** Heart & Small Intestine
- **Chakra Influence:** Heart Chakra, Crown Chakra
- **Emotion:** Joy (when flowing), restlessness or anxiety (when imbalanced)
- **Elemental Wisdom:** Fire is the spark of inspiration, love, and joyful expression. It's the warmth of laughter, the radiance of connection, and the courage to show up fully. Balanced Fire energy brings vitality, charisma, and emotional openness. Imbalanced Fire may lead to emotional instability, overwhelm, or burnout. Reiki supports Fire by calming the nervous system and reigniting authentic joy.

Earth – The Ground of Nourishment and Stability

- **Season:** Late Summer / Transition Seasons
- **Organs:** Spleen & Stomach
- **Chakra Influence:** Root Chakra, Solar Plexus
- **Emotion:** Worry or overthinking (when imbalanced), empathy (when balanced)
- **Elemental Wisdom:** Earth is the center, the caregiver, the nurturer. It provides structure, support, and the ability to digest both food and life's experiences. When Earth energy is strong, we feel grounded, generous, and safe. Imbalance may manifest as clinginess, brain fog, or emotional co-dependency.

Reiki brings Earth back into balance by calming mental chatter, strengthening boundaries, and restoring the center.

Metal – The Precision of Letting Go and Refinement

- **Season:** Autumn
- **Organs:** Lungs & Large Intestine
- **Chakra Influence:** Throat Chakra, Third Eye
- **Emotion:** Grief (when blocked), inspiration and clarity (when balanced)
- **Elemental Wisdom:** Metal is the alchemist—it purifies, clarifies, and teaches us what to keep and what to release. Metal energy helps us set boundaries, breathe deeply, and embrace change. When imbalanced, grief may be unexpressed, or we may become overly critical, rigid, or detached. Reiki supports Metal energy by releasing emotional weight, encouraging clarity, and allowing space for breath and spirit to move freely.

Water – The Depth of Stillness and Intuition

- **Season:** Winter
- **Organs:** Kidneys & Bladder
- **Chakra Influence:** Sacral Chakra, Root Chakra
- **Emotion:** Fear (when imbalanced), wisdom and trust (when balanced)
- **Elemental Wisdom:** Water is the philosopher, the dreamer, the keeper of mysteries. It governs rest, intuition, and the deep inner current of life. When balanced, Water grants access to creativity, resilience, and spiritual insight. Imbalance may manifest as fear,

exhaustion, or emotional withdrawal. Reiki nourishes Water by restoring inner calm, encouraging surrender, and reconnecting us with our intuitive flow.

These five elements are not fixed personalities—they are flowing archetypes that move through us depending on our life stage, emotional state, health, and environment. One day we may feel fiery and social, the next quiet and watery. And that's the beauty of it: **we are never just one thing**.

When we integrate Reiki with the Five Elements, we begin to sense which energy is lacking, which is overactive, and which needs attention—not through diagnosis, but through intuition. As your awareness of each element grows, your Reiki sessions become more attuned to nature's rhythms, your client's emotional patterns, and your own energetic needs.

The Five Elements in the Body and Beyond

Corresponding Seasons, Organs, Emotions, Senses, and Colors

Each of the Five Elements is more than an energetic pattern—it is a **whole system of relationships**. These elements are connected to **every aspect of human experience**: the rhythms of the seasons, the functioning of our organs, the depth of our emotions, the way we perceive the world through our senses, and even the colors that influence our energetic vibration.

Understanding these correspondences allows Reiki practitioners to recognize subtle energetic imbalances and bring intentional healing to the body, mind, and spirit. Let's explore the full energetic profile of each element.

Wood

- **Season:** Spring – the season of renewal, movement, and vision.
- **Organs:** Liver (yin), Gallbladder (yang) – responsible for detoxification, decision-making, and emotional flow.
- **Emotion:** Anger (unbalanced), assertiveness and purpose (balanced).
- **Sense:** Sight – connected to clarity of vision, insight, and perception.
- **Color:** Green – the color of new growth, harmony, and life force.
- **Energetic Vibe:** "I grow. I expand. I create direction."

Conscious breathwork and focused mantras help direct and amplify the flow of energy, promote balance and emotional release.

Fire

- **Season:** Summer – the time of joy, full expression, and connection.
- **Organs:** Heart (yin), Small Intestine (yang) – guardians of emotion, circulation, and inner truth.
- **Emotion:** Joy (balanced), anxiety or mania (unbalanced).
- **Sense:** Speech (via the tongue) – expression of truth and heartfelt connection.
- **Color:** Red – symbolizes passion, life force, warmth, and vitality.
- **Energetic Vibe:** "I love. I connect. I radiate."

Earth

- **Season:** Late Summer – or the transitional phase between seasons; a time of nourishment and stability.
- **Organs:** Spleen (yin), Stomach (yang) – associated with digestion, assimilation (of food and life), and mental clarity.
- **Emotion:** Worry or overthinking (unbalanced), compassion and centeredness (balanced).
- **Sense:** Taste – relating to nourishment, sweetness, and satisfaction.
- **Color:** Yellow – the color of grounded joy, stability, and clarity.
- **Energetic Vibe:** "I nurture. I support. I remain steady."

Metal

- **Season:** Autumn – the time of reflection, refinement, and letting go.
- **Organs:** Lungs (yin), Large Intestine (yang) – governing breath, boundaries, and elimination.
- **Emotion:** Grief or detachment (unbalanced), reverence and clarity (balanced).
- **Sense:** Smell – linked to memory, subtle perception, and instinct.
- **Color:** White or Silver – associated with purity, illumination, and precision.
- **Energetic Vibe:** "I release. I refine. I find truth."

Water

- **Season:** Winter – the season of rest, reflection, and deep restoration.
- **Organs:** Kidneys (yin), Bladder (yang) – the roots of life force, governing vitality, fear, and wisdom.
- **Emotion:** Fear or withdrawal (unbalanced), courage and inner knowing (balanced).
- **Sense:** Hearing – connected to inner listening, intuition, and resonance.
- **Color:** Blue or Black – representing depth, introspection, and stillness.
- **Energetic Vibe:** "I feel. I listen. I surrender."

These elemental correspondences are more than symbolic— they are **living guides** that help you sense and respond to energetic needs. When a client comes to you feeling lost, you may sense an imbalance in **Wood**. When someone feels emotionally numb, **Fire** may be diminished. When they can't

Conscious breathwork and focused mantras help direct and amplify the flow of energy, promote balance and emotional release.

let go of a past experience, it may be **Metal** calling for attention.

By layering this knowledge with Reiki's intuitive flow, your healing sessions become **personalized, nature-informed, and profoundly aligned** with the rhythms of life.

Elemental Imbalances: Excess and Deficiency

Reading the Body Through the Language of Nature

In the same way the weather shifts—too much rain, too little sun—our inner elemental energies can become unbalanced. These imbalances are not just metaphysical concepts; they show up in very real ways: physically, emotionally, mentally, and spiritually.

Each element, when in harmony, provides its gifts with ease: clarity, creativity, rest, joy, strength. But when an element is in **excess**, it overwhelms the system; when in **deficiency**, it creates weakness or stagnation.

Learning to recognize these patterns is at the heart of elemental Reiki. The more you understand the language of imbalance, the more precisely you can bring healing energy where it is most needed.

Wood Imbalance

- **Excess Wood:** Irritability, impatience, controlling behavior, high blood pressure, tension in the muscles (especially the neck and shoulders).
- **Deficient Wood:** Lack of direction, procrastination, indecision, low motivation, weak digestion, poor vision.
- **What it needs:** Flow, clarity, boundaries, and healthy expression of emotions—especially anger.

Conscious breathwork and focused mantras help direct and amplify the flow of energy, promoting balance and emotional release.

Fire Imbalance

- **Excess Fire:** Anxiety, restlessness, insomnia, manic energy, over-talking, over-sharing, racing thoughts.
- **Deficient Fire:** Emotional numbness, isolation, lack of joy, fatigue, poor circulation, difficulty connecting with others.
- **What it needs:** Balanced heart energy, inner joy, calm presence, and authentic connection.

Earth Imbalance

- **Excess Earth:** Over-caregiving, codependency, obsession with security, overthinking, digestive issues (bloating, heaviness).
- **Deficient Earth:** Spaciness, inability to focus, feeling unsupported, poor appetite, unstable mood.
- **What it needs:** Grounding, self-nourishment, routine, and healthy emotional digestion.

Metal Imbalance

- **Excess Metal:** Rigid thinking, perfectionism, judgment, emotional detachment, chronic respiratory issues.
- **Deficient Metal:** Difficulty letting go, unresolved grief, low self-worth, cluttered thinking, weak immunity.
- **What it needs:** Breath, release, clarity, reverence for the past—and the ability to move forward.

Water Imbalance

- **Excess Water:** Withdrawal, excessive fear, paranoia, hormonal imbalance, coldness (physically and emotionally).
- **Deficient Water:** Burnout, low back pain, adrenal fatigue, lack of willpower, inability to rest or regenerate.
- **What it needs:** Deep rest, inner stillness, replenishment, and the return of trust—especially in oneself.

These imbalances don't exist in isolation. A deficiency in one element often leads to excess in another. For instance, **deficient Water** (fatigue, fear, low reserves) may lead to **excess Fire** (burnout, anxiety) as the body overcompensates. Similarly, **excess Earth** (overthinking, emotional heaviness) may suppress **Wood's** natural desire for growth and movement.

This is where Reiki becomes more than a healing tool—it becomes a **balancing art**. Your hands, your awareness, and your intuition become the instruments through which nature can restore itself.

Conscious breathwork and focused mantras help direct and amplify the flow of energy, promote balance and emotional release.

Chapter 3: Where Reiki and the Five Elements Intersect

Energy Channels – Meridians vs. Chakras

If Reiki is the current, then our energy systems are the **rivers** and **reservoirs** through which it flows.

As a Reiki practitioner, you are already familiar with the **chakra system**—the seven main energy centers that align along the spine, each corresponding to physical, emotional, and spiritual aspects of our being. When balanced, the chakras spin freely, allowing life force energy (Reiki) to circulate through the body with ease. But blockages, emotional trauma, and stress can cause these centers to become overactive, sluggish, or completely shut down.

In Traditional Chinese Medicine (TCM), the body is seen through a different yet equally powerful lens—one shaped by the **meridian system**. Meridians are **invisible energy pathways** that run throughout the body like highways, connecting organs, emotions, and elemental energies. These channels carry **Qi** (life force) and are stimulated through acupuncture, acupressure, qigong, and yes—even Reiki.

Where chakras are more like **central power hubs**, meridians are the **distribution lines**. One is vertical (chakras), and the other is horizontal and web-like (meridians). One is more esoteric and rooted in Indian yogic traditions, while the other is based on thousands of years of Chinese medical observation and energetic mapping.

But the truth is—they are not in opposition. They are **complementary languages of the same energetic body**.

The Chakra System: The Vertical Axis of Transformation

- Consists of **seven major chakras** (plus minor chakras) aligned with the spinal column.
- Each chakra is associated with a **color, element, emotion, sound, organ**, and **spiritual lesson**.
- Energy flows from the **Root (Earth connection)** to the **Crown (Divine connection)**—bridging body and spirit.

In Reiki, we often place our hands on or near these centers to clear, balance, and activate the flow of energy. As you may have experienced, even slight energetic shifts in a single chakra can lead to profound emotional or physical relief.

The Meridian System: The Web of Elemental Flow

- Contains **12 primary meridians**, each paired with an organ and corresponding **yin or yang** energy.
- Flows are **cyclical**—moving in a 24-hour pattern known as the **Chinese Body Clock**.
- Meridians reflect the **Five Elements**, with each pair representing an aspect of nature and emotional experience.

Conscious breathwork and focused mantras help direct and amplify the flow of energy, promote balance and emotional release.

For example:

- The **Liver and Gallbladder meridians** correspond to **Wood**, governing vision, planning, and stored anger.
- The **Heart and Small Intestine** relate to **Fire**, overseeing joy, expression, and connection.
- The **Lungs and Large Intestine** are part of **Metal**, helping us breathe, release, and grieve.

When energy becomes stagnant in a meridian, it may not immediately show in the chakras, but symptoms arise in the corresponding organs or emotions. Reiki, when applied with awareness of these pathways, can gently stimulate movement along the meridians—unblocking the energetic rivers and restoring elemental flow.

Where They Intersect: Your Healing Advantage

Imagine this: you're working on a client's **heart chakra**—their chest feels tight, their breath shallow, and they're holding back tears. You intuitively know they're grieving something unspoken. Now, add in your understanding of the **Lung meridian** (Metal element), which runs through the chest and governs the energy of **grief, breath, and release**.

By focusing Reiki energy not just on the chakra, but also along the meridian pathways, you create a **multi-dimensional healing experience**. You're addressing the energetic blockage **vertically (chakra)** and **horizontally (meridian)**—meeting the client where they are in their emotional, physical, and elemental journey.

This integration is what makes Elemental Reiki so powerful. You are no longer working with chakras *or* meridians—you're working with **the whole energetic ecosystem**.

As you move forward in this book, you'll begin to explore how to assess elemental and energetic imbalances using both systems. You'll learn how to align your Reiki hand placements with meridian flow, chakra resonance, and elemental wisdom.

Energy doesn't compartmentalize—and neither should healing.

Conscious breathwork and focused mantras help direct and amplify the flow of energy, promot
balance and emotional release.

Emotional Energy: Where the Elements Meet the Chakras

Understanding the Emotional Landscape of Elemental Reiki

In both Reiki and the Five Element system, **emotion is energy in motion**—a vital part of our life force that must move freely in order for us to feel healthy, balanced, and whole. Just as water must flow and fire must burn, emotions must be acknowledged, processed, and expressed.

When emotions are suppressed or over-amplified, they create blockages—not just mentally, but physically and energetically. This stagnation can settle in the **chakras** or **meridians**, influencing everything from posture and breath to relationships and purpose.

By understanding which **elemental emotion** resides within each **chakra**, you can begin to see your clients—and yourself—with deeper insight and compassion. You'll be able to sense when an emotion is calling for release, balance, or support—and guide your Reiki healing accordingly.

Root Chakra (Earth + Water)

- **Elemental Emotions:** Fear (Water) + Worry (Earth)
- **When Blocked:** Insecurity, survival anxiety, mistrust, chronic tension, fatigue.
- **Reiki Focus:** Grounding hand positions, soothing breathwork, safety-based affirmations.

- **Supportive Tools:** Stones like hematite or black tourmaline, grounding oils like cedarwood, deep touch.

Sacral Chakra (Water)

- **Elemental Emotion:** Fear, especially of vulnerability, change, or abandonment.
- **When Blocked:** Creative suppression, emotional numbness, intimacy issues, guilt.
- **Reiki Focus:** Gentle flow-based handwork, movement-based meditations, releasing stuck emotional energy.
- **Supportive Tools:** Warm water baths, moonstone, clary sage, creative journaling.

Solar Plexus (Wood + Fire)

- **Elemental Emotions:** Anger (Wood) + Shame or Anxiety (Fire when imbalanced)
- **When Blocked:** Low self-esteem, control issues, overthinking, digestive imbalance.
- **Reiki Focus:** Energizing techniques, chakra rotation, visualization of personal power.
- **Supportive Tools:** Lemon essential oil, tiger's eye, journaling on boundaries and self-worth.

Heart Chakra (Fire + Earth)

- **Elemental Emotions:** Joy (Fire) + Compassion/Worry (Earth)
- **When Blocked:** Grief, emotional walls, co-dependency, loneliness.

Conscious breathwork and focused mantras help direct and amplify the flow of energy, promoting balance and emotional release.

- **Reiki Focus:** Gentle chest work, breath alignment, forgiveness energy.
- **Supportive Tools:** Rose quartz, rose oil, self-love affirmations, gratitude practices.

Throat Chakra (Metal)

- **Elemental Emotion:** Grief
- **When Blocked:** Difficulty speaking truth, repressed sadness, throat or respiratory issues.
- **Reiki Focus:** Hovering hands or light touch at the throat and upper chest, releasing rituals.
- **Supportive Tools:** Peppermint oil, lapis lazuli, journaling unspoken thoughts.

Third Eye Chakra (Wood + Metal)

- **Elemental Emotions:** Anger (Wood when suppressed) + Grief (Metal when unresolved)
- **When Blocked:** Lack of vision, confusion, spiritual disconnection, over-analysis.
- **Reiki Focus:** Light touch or no-touch method at the forehead, inner vision meditations.
- **Supportive Tools:** Amethyst, frankincense, dreamwork, visualization exercises.

Crown Chakra (Metal + Water)

- **Elemental Emotions:** Fear (Water of the unknown) + Grief (Metal of detachment from the divine)
- **When Blocked:** Spiritual isolation, closed-mindedness, chronic worry about purpose.

- **Reiki Focus:** Quiet, receptive energy work; holding space rather than directing energy.
- **Supportive Tools:** Quartz crystal, lavender oil, silent reflection, open sky visualization.

Why This Matters in Reiki Practice

When you understand that each **chakra holds an elemental emotion**, you no longer see anger as "bad" or grief as something to suppress—you see them as **messages from nature**, showing you where energy is trying to move. You become a listener, a translator, and a guide.

Reiki doesn't force emotions to change—it creates a safe, loving space where energy can reorganize itself. By aligning your hand placements, intentions, and elemental awareness, you give each chakra what it needs—not to be "fixed," but to come home to itself.

Conscious breathwork and focused mantras help direct and amplify the flow of energy, promote balance and emotional release.

Case Examples: Rebalancing the Elements with Reiki

Real Stories of Element-Based Healing

As we've explored, elemental energy is woven into every aspect of our lives—our health, our emotions, our thoughts, and our spiritual state. When an element is out of balance, it manifests uniquely in each person: sometimes subtly, sometimes dramatically. Reiki, when applied with elemental awareness, becomes more than a technique—it becomes an intuitive, holistic art of rebalancing nature within the body.

Let's take a look at a few real-life examples where Elemental Reiki helped restore harmony and flow.

Case 1: The Angry, Burnt-Out Entrepreneur (Wood + Fire Imbalance)

Client Profile: Mid-30s male, high-achieving business owner, reports frustration, digestive issues, tension in shoulders, poor sleep.

Elemental Imbalance: Excess Wood (anger, control) + Deficient Fire (burnout, emotional detachment)

Chakras affected: Solar Plexus, Heart, and Third Eye
Reiki Focus:

- Began with grounding Root and Solar Plexus to stabilize and drain excess Wood energy.
- Focused on Heart Chakra to reignite joy and connection with Fire element.

- Used calming hand placements over the liver area and a short visualization of a forest slowly being restored.

Result: After three sessions, the client reported improved sleep, clearer communication with his team, less tension in the shoulders, and a surprising return of creative ideas.

Case 2: The Overgiver with No Boundaries (Earth + Metal Imbalance)

Client Profile: Female Reiki Level I student, caregiver, struggles with chronic fatigue, digestive bloating, and persistent sadness she couldn't explain.
Elemental Imbalance: Excess Earth (over-nurturing) + Deficient Metal (inability to release)

Chakras affected: Solar Plexus, Throat, and Root
Reiki Focus:

- Supported Earth energy with gentle touch at Solar Plexus and Root for grounding and strength.
- Cleared stagnant energy in the Lungs and Throat using hover techniques, encouraging emotional release.
- Added affirmations for self-worth and boundaries, along with journaling prompts on "What am I ready to let go of?"

Result: The client began setting healthier limits with others, noticed improvements in digestion, and reported that tears flowed naturally during her second session—a major emotional breakthrough.

Conscious breathwork and focused mantras help direct and amplify the flow of energy, promot balance and emotional release.

Case 3: The Frozen Creative (Water Deficiency, Fire Excess)

Client Profile: Young female artist, highly intuitive but overwhelmed by anxiety and chronic fatigue, creative blocks, fear of being seen.
Elemental Imbalance: Deficient Water (no reserves) + Overactive Fire (burnout, emotional dysregulation)

Chakras affected: Sacral, Crown, and Heart
Reiki Focus:

- Sessions focused on Sacral Chakra and Kidney meridian to restore flow and nourish Water element.
- Cooling Reiki techniques (hovering, slow breathwork) used to calm Fire energy.
- Encouraged visualization of water gently moving through her creative space and a journaling ritual involving her dreams.

Result: The client regained her creative rhythm, reported reduced anxiety, and began painting again after months of creative silence.

Case 4: The Grieving Widow (Metal Imbalance, Throat Blockage)

Client Profile: Elderly woman, recently lost her spouse, struggling with chest heaviness, shallow breathing, and frequent sore throats.
Elemental Imbalance: Stagnant Metal (grief not expressed)
Chakras affected: Throat, Heart, and Lungs

Reiki Focus:

- Gentle energy work at the chest and throat, holding space for unspoken emotion.
- Use of breath-based Reiki techniques to open Lung meridians.
- She was invited to speak her late husband's name aloud during a session and say what she wished she could tell him.

Result: Emotional release came with tears and a sense of peace. In the following weeks, her breathing improved, and her voice carried more strength and clarity.

The Takeaway

These case examples reflect something powerful: **you don't need to diagnose to heal—you only need to listen**. By tuning into elemental patterns and aligning them with Reiki's intelligent flow, you become a translator of energy, a guide back to harmony.

Each client is a unique landscape—some needing more fire, others more earth, some simply needing water to return to the roots of their being. The Five Elements give you the lens. Reiki gives you the light.

Conscious breathwork and focused mantras help direct and amplify the flow of energy, promo
balance and emotional release.

Creating Personalized Reiki Sessions Using Element Theory

Tailoring Healing to the Rhythm of Nature

No two people are the same—and neither are any two Reiki sessions.

When you integrate the Five Element Theory into your Reiki practice, you move from a one-size-fits-all approach to one that is **deeply intuitive, seasonal, and energetically aligned**. Each element brings its own wisdom, its own message, and its own way of expressing disharmony in the body, emotions, or spirit.

By identifying the dominant **elemental imbalance**, you can create sessions that not only balance the chakras but restore harmony on a deeper, more natural level—supporting the client in returning to their *true energetic rhythm*.

Step 1: Determine the Elemental Imbalance

Before beginning a session, take a few moments to assess where your client (or you, if it's self-Reiki) may be out of balance. You can use:

- Physical symptoms
- Emotional states
- Recent life challenges
- Seasonal influences
- Chakra or meridian cues

- Responses from a pre-session questionnaire or intuitive guidance

Ask:

- What emotions are most present?
- What area of the body is calling attention?
- Are they feeling drained or overactive in any area of life?
- What season or life phase are they in?

For example:

- Excess **Fire** may show as restlessness, burnout, or insomnia.
- Deficient **Earth** might show as worry, digestive issues, or a sense of instability.
- Stagnant **Metal** could appear as unresolved grief or difficulty letting go.

Step 2: Choose the Elemental Focus

Once the imbalance is identified, set your intention and choose the **elemental energy** you want to bring into harmony.

Ask:

- Do I need to calm, nourish, or stimulate this energy?
- Which chakras are related to this element?
- What tools (oils, crystals, colors, breathwork) might support this element?

Conscious breathwork and focused mantras help direct and amplify the flow of energy, promote balance and emotional release.

Each element corresponds to particular organs, chakras, and emotions, giving you a clear energetic "map" to guide your session. (You can refer back to the earlier chapters or use a printed elemental chart.)

Step 3: Customize the Reiki Flow

Use traditional Reiki hand positions as your foundation, but adapt the session based on the element. Here's how:

For Excess Energy (Element is Overactive):

- Use **hovering hands**, light touch, or pull-away techniques to draw off energy.
- Focus on **grounding** and **calming** the system.
- Support with **deep breathing**, slow pacing, and quiet stillness.

For Deficient Energy (Element is Weak or Depleted):

- Use **steady, focused touch** to nourish and hold space.
- Channel energy with **intention and warmth**.
- Use affirmations, colors, or oils that **build** rather than release.

Step 4: Integrate Elemental Tools

Adding simple elemental support tools can elevate the energy and anchor the healing:

- **Crystals:** Choose based on element (e.g., red jasper for Earth, aquamarine for Water)
- **Essential oils:** Use scent to reinforce the element (e.g., rosemary for Wood, lavender for Fire)

- **Color therapy:** Drape a scarf or place a colored cloth over the area of imbalance
- **Affirmations:** Speak or have the client silently repeat statements aligned with the needed element
- **Sound or breath:** Match rhythm with elemental qualities (e.g., flowing breath for Water, sharp exhale for Metal)

Step 5: Reflect and Release

After the session, encourage integration. Ask the client (or journal for yourself):

- What came up emotionally or physically?
- Did a memory or image surface?
- What element feels most present now?
- What simple self-care or ritual might help continue the balancing process?

Even something as simple as drinking herbal tea related to the element (e.g., peppermint for Metal, chamomile for Earth) or stepping outside into a seasonally aligned environment can extend the healing energy beyond the table.

The Elemental Reiki Practitioner's Gift

When you create sessions rooted in elemental wisdom, you don't just treat symptoms—you **speak the language of nature**. You help people feel seen, heard, and aligned—not only with their inner self but with the world around them.

Conscious breathwork and focused mantras help direct and amplify the flow of energy, promote balance and emotional release.

You become a bridge between heaven and earth, spirit and body, intuition and action. And that is the true gift of Elemental Reiki.

PART 2:
ELEMENTAL REIKI
IN PRACTICE

Conscious breathwork and focused mantras help direct and amplify the flow of energy, promote balance and emotional release.

Chapter 4: Water Element – The Power of Flow & Fear

Season: Winter – The Wisdom of Stillness

Winter is the season of silence, reflection, and deep restoration. Nature slows down. Trees conserve their energy. Animals retreat into stillness. And beneath the frozen surface, life is quietly gathering its strength.

The **Water Element** mirrors this sacred pause. It asks us to go inward, to rest, and to listen to the quiet voice within. In Traditional Chinese Medicine, Winter is a time to **preserve energy**, not expend it—a time to embrace **being over doing**, and **depth over surface**.

But in modern life, this wisdom is often ignored. We push through, even as our bodies beg for rest. We resist the call to slow down, fearing what might rise from the stillness. And yet, it's in this slowing that healing begins.

Winter teaches us the **value of emptiness**—not as lack, but as potential. Just as seeds lie dormant beneath the snow, so too do our deepest insights and untapped strength, waiting for the right conditions to emerge.

In Reiki practice, aligning with the Winter season means honoring the quiet. Your sessions may feel slower, more introspective, and deeply grounding. Clients may bring forward themes of exhaustion, fear, or uncertainty. These are not signs of weakness—but invitations to soften, surrender, and restore.

When we work with Reiki during Winter, we support the **Water Element** by encouraging:

- Stillness in the body and breath
- Reconnection to the Root and Sacral Chakras
- A sense of safety in the unknown
- Courage to face inner fears
- Trust in divine timing

Let your hands be still. Let your energy be soft. Let your presence be a sanctuary.

For in Winter, doing less **is** doing more. And from this sacred stillness, true strength is born.

Conscious breathwork and focused mantras help direct and amplify the flow of energy, promote balance and emotional release.

Organs: Kidneys & Bladder – The Reservoir of Life Force

In the system of Traditional Chinese Medicine, the **Kidneys** are considered the **gatekeepers of life force**, storing the vital essence known as *Jing*. They are more than just physical organs; they are the deep well of our **resilience, vitality, and ancestral energy**. When Kidney energy is strong, we feel rooted, fearless, and capable of navigating life's unknowns. When it is depleted, we feel fragile, anxious, overwhelmed— or as if life itself is slipping through our fingers.

The **Bladder**, paired with the Kidneys as its yang counterpart, acts as the body's energetic filtration system. It governs the **ability to eliminate waste**, both physically and emotionally. A sluggish or imbalanced Bladder system may manifest as **holding onto fear**, past trauma, or the emotional residue of stress.

Together, the Kidneys and Bladder form the energetic foundation of the **Water Element**. They govern:

- **Rest and regeneration**
- **Courage and fear**
- **Longevity and life purpose**
- **Reproductive health, bones, ears, and lower back**

Common signs of Water Element disharmony often appear through these organs:

- Fatigue that rest doesn't fix
- Frequent urination or water retention

- Lower back pain or stiffness
- Hormonal imbalance
- Heightened fear, anxiety, or panic
- Feeling emotionally "frozen" or depleted

In Reiki practice, focusing on these organs supports the body's **deepest reserves**. When you place your hands over the lower back (Kidneys) or lower abdomen (Bladder/Sacral Chakra), you're not just offering comfort—you're reminding the body how to restore itself at the most primal level.

Reiki in this area helps:

- Replenish drained energy stores
- Restore trust and emotional safety
- Quiet the mind
- Support fertility and sexual vitality
- Release fear gently and gradually

When we support the Kidneys and Bladder with Reiki, we are honoring the **sacred root of vitality**—the place where courage is born, and from which the rest of life can begin to flow again.

Conscious breathwork and focused mantras help direct and amplify the flow of energy, promote balance and emotional release.

Chakras: Root & Sacral – Anchors of Safety and Flow

The Water Element finds its home at the base of the body— in the Root and Sacral Chakras, where your connection to the physical world and your emotional depths reside. These two energy centers form the foundation of your energetic body, and when they are in harmony, they create a powerful sense of safety, flow, and inner knowing.

Root Chakra – Muladhara

Located at the base of the spine, the Root Chakra is associated with survival, stability, and trust. It reflects your sense of safety in the world—physically, emotionally, and energetically.

When the Water Element is imbalanced, the Root Chakra often expresses it through:

- Persistent fear or anxiety
- Difficulty feeling grounded or "in your body"
- Money or security worries
- Lower back pain or cold extremities

Reiki at the Root Chakra can soothe fear, calm the nervous system, and restore a sense of presence and belonging. Gentle, steady hand placements over the tailbone, hips, or soles of the feet encourage reconnection with the Earth and self.

Sacral Chakra – Svadhisthana

Located just below the navel, the Sacral Chakra governs **emotion, creativity, sensuality, and flow**. It is the energy of movement—of both water and life.

When the Water Element is imbalanced, you may experience:

- Difficulty processing or expressing emotion
- Creative blockages
- Fear of intimacy or rejection
- Fluid imbalances, reproductive issues, or bladder problems

Reiki over the Sacral Chakra gently unlocks this stagnant energy, allowing emotional expression and creative flow to return. It helps **release shame**, **ease fear**, and **reignite joy** in the body.

Together, the Root and Sacral Chakras form the **energetic basin of the Water Element**. When balanced, they help you feel **safe enough to let go**—to surrender control, to trust life's flow, and to navigate uncertainty with grounded confidence.

As a practitioner, when you work with these chakras using Reiki and elemental awareness, you are not only helping to rebalance energy—you are **restoring the emotional foundation of courage**.

Conscious breathwork and focused mantras help direct and amplify the flow of energy, promo balance and emotional release.

Emotion: Fear – The Wisdom Within the Unknown

Of all the elemental emotions, **fear** is the most primal. It lives in the body like water lives in the Earth—deep, powerful, often unseen, yet shaping everything it touches.

In the Water Element, fear is not the enemy—it is the **teacher**. It alerts us to danger, sharpens our instincts, and calls us to listen. But when left unacknowledged, fear becomes distorted. It begins to control us, freeze us, or quietly erode our sense of trust in life.

Fear shows up in many forms:

- Fear of failure
- Fear of success
- Fear of abandonment
- Fear of the unknown
- Fear of being seen
- Fear of change

Unlike other emotions that flare and pass, fear lingers. It hides in the background, tightening muscles, quickening breath, and disrupting the flow of energy in the Root and Sacral Chakras. Left unchecked, fear can **drain the Kidneys**, exhaust the nervous system, and create a chronic feeling of being unsafe—even when nothing is "wrong."

But fear also holds a sacred message:

"It's time to pause. Listen. Reconnect with your power."

When we work with fear through the lens of Reiki and the Water Element, we don't try to push it away. We hold it. We **create space** for it to soften. We breathe with it, offering reassurance and energetic support.

Reiki allows you to gently:

- Invite fear to the surface without judgment
- Witness the body's response and calm the nervous system
- Re-establish trust in the self and in the unknown
- Transform fear into courage—not by force, but through *presence*

As a practitioner or self-healer, remember: fear is part of the human experience. It is not a flaw to be fixed, but an energy to be honored and redirected.

When the Water Element is balanced, fear transforms into its higher expression: **wisdom**. You become still enough to hear your inner voice. You develop quiet courage. You begin to trust the timing of your life.

And like the river that carves through stone, you remember:

Flow is stronger than force.

Conscious breathwork and focused mantras help direct and amplify the flow of energy, promote balance and emotional release.

Reiki Practice for Grounding and Courage

Calling Back Strength Through the Water Element

When the Water Element is out of balance, we often feel **adrift**—ungrounded, fearful, or disconnected from our inner reserves. The nervous system may be overactive, the body fatigued, the breath shallow. In these moments, Reiki becomes a **safe container**—a sanctuary where the mind can slow down, the body can soften, and courage can begin to return.

This practice supports the **Kidneys, Bladder, Root and Sacral Chakras**, and the emotional frequency of fear. It is best used during times of anxiety, exhaustion, emotional numbness, or after periods of prolonged stress or uncertainty.

Preparation

- Create a **quiet, dimly lit space**—preferably with soft music, a cozy blanket, and grounding elements (stones, candles, warm tea).
- Sit or lie down in a comfortable position with your spine supported.
- Set a clear **intention**, such as:
  "I allow fear to soften. I am safe to feel. I restore my inner strength."

Step-by-Step Practice

1. **Start with the Breath**
   Begin by placing one hand on your **lower belly** and one on your **chest**. Breathe slowly and deeply.
   Inhale to a count of 4, hold for 2, and exhale for 6.
   Let your breath move like water—fluid and gentle.

2. **Root Chakra Hold**
   Place both hands over your **pelvis or upper thighs**, or imagine anchoring roots into the Earth.
   Visualize deep red light expanding with each breath.
   As you hold this position, mentally affirm:
   "I am safe. I am held. I belong."

3. **Kidney Hold**
   Move your hands to your **lower back**, just above the waist on either side of the spine.
   Feel warmth gathering here—like heated water filling a reservoir.
   Visualize deep indigo or midnight blue light pulsing softly.
   Affirm:
   "My energy is replenished. I trust life's flow."

4. **Sacral Chakra Flow**
   Bring your hands to your **lower abdomen**—just below the navel.
   Imagine water swirling gently in this space. Let any emotion rise and fall like a wave.
   You may silently repeat:
   "It is safe to feel. My emotions move with ease."

5. **Complete with Grounding**
   Place your hands on the **soles of your feet** or visualize energy anchoring into the earth.
   Feel the connection between your body and the world

Conscious breathwork and focused mantras help direct and amplify the flow of energy, promote balance and emotional release.

beneath you.
Rest here until you feel centered and complete.

Integration

After your session, drink a glass of warm water or herbal tea (such as licorice root or chamomile). Journal or reflect on anything that surfaced. You may feel lighter, quieter, or more aware of what needs release.

Reiki is not about "fixing" fear—it is about **befriending it**, holding space for it to loosen its grip, and calling back your inner strength with compassion.

The more often you work with Reiki and the Water Element, the more deeply you will trust your ability to flow—even through uncertainty.

Water Element Affirmations

(Winter | Kidneys & Bladder | Root & Sacral | Emotion: Fear)

1. *I am safe to be still. I trust the wisdom in the quiet.*
2. *I release fear and embrace flow.*
3. *My energy is replenished with each breath.*
4. *I surrender control and allow life to guide me.*
5. *Even in darkness, I am whole and protected.*

Chapter 5: Wood Element – Growth, Anger & Direction

Season: Spring – The Season of Emergence and Expansion

Spring is the season of **awakening**—when nature shakes off the weight of winter and bursts into life with vibrant, determined energy. Seeds sprout, trees bud, and the Earth stretches toward the sun in an upward spiral of growth.

This is the **essence of the Wood Element**: expansion, direction, and the unstoppable drive to become. Just as trees push through the soil after months of stillness, our own energy stirs in spring, encouraging us to take action, make decisions, and pursue our purpose with clarity and confidence.

But growth isn't always graceful. As sap rises and energy accelerates, tension can build. Impatience, frustration, and irritability are common during this time—especially when our plans feel blocked or our path is unclear. In this way, Spring also surfaces **emotional residue** that winter's stillness may have hidden. What lies dormant must now move.

Conscious breathwork and focused mantras help direct and amplify the flow of energy, promote balance and emotional release.

Reiki sessions in the spring often reflect this shift. Clients may report tight muscles, mood swings, migraines, or a sense of "pent-up" energy. Spiritually, they may feel driven to change but unsure how. This is the perfect moment to support the Wood Element with energy work that encourages **release, movement, and direction**.

By aligning your Reiki practice with Spring's rising rhythm, you help guide energy where it longs to go—**forward**.

When you honor the Wood Element in Spring, you affirm this sacred truth:

"I am allowed to grow. I am allowed to change. I am allowed to move forward."

Organs: Liver & Gallbladder – The Architects of Vision and Action

In Traditional Chinese Medicine, the **Liver** and **Gallbladder** are the primary organs associated with the **Wood Element**. Together, they form a dynamic duo—responsible for transforming vision into action, and stagnation into flow.

The **Liver** is seen as the body's **master planner**. It governs not only the smooth flow of blood and Qi, but also the flow of **emotions, ideas, and life force**. It helps you envision your path, make decisions, and adapt to obstacles with creativity and flexibility. When Liver energy is in balance, you feel clear, directed, and able to grow without resistance.

The **Gallbladder**, the Liver's yang partner, governs **decision-making, courage, and assertiveness**. It helps you take decisive action without hesitation or fear of failure. When its energy is strong, you trust yourself and move forward with clarity.

When the Wood Element is **excessive**, these organs become **overstimulated**, leading to symptoms like:

- Irritability or sudden bursts of anger
- Tension in the neck, shoulders, or jaw
- Headaches, migraines, or eye strain
- Digestive issues, especially related to fats
- PMS or hormonal imbalance

Conscious breathwork and focused mantras help direct and amplify the flow of energy, promote balance and emotional release.

When deficient, Wood energy may present as:

- Indecision or procrastination
- Feeling stuck or directionless
- Fatigue and lack of motivation
- Depression masked as apathy or withdrawal

In both cases, the Liver and Gallbladder need support—not to be "forced" into flow, but to be **gently encouraged** with the help of Reiki, breath, movement, and emotional release.

Reiki over the **right ribcage (Liver)** or along the **gallbladder meridian** (which runs from the side of the head down to the outer leg) can help ease tension, restore clarity, and reestablish **emotional flexibility**. When these organs are supported, the body feels more spacious—and the soul feels free to grow again.

The Liver gives you **vision**. The Gallbladder gives you the **guts** to follow it.

Chakra: Solar Plexus – The Seat of Power and Purpose

The **Solar Plexus Chakra**, known as **Manipura** in Sanskrit, is the energetic center of **willpower, self-esteem, personal identity, and action**. It is the fire in your belly—the place where dreams transform into decisions, and intentions become movement.

In the context of the **Wood Element**, the Solar Plexus functions like the sun rising over the forest—it fuels growth, clears confusion, and shines light on the next step forward. This chakra governs your ability to set boundaries, make confident choices, and stand in your truth.

When Wood energy is **excessive**, the Solar Plexus may become **overactive**:

- You may feel intense internal pressure to act or control.
- You might lash out in frustration, become overly rigid, or struggle with anger.
- The body may tense—especially in the abdomen, diaphragm, and shoulders.

When Wood energy is **deficient**, this chakra may become **weak or blocked**:

- You may feel lost, indecisive, or unsure of your next step.
- Self-doubt or fear of judgment may take hold.

Conscious breathwork and focused mantras help direct and amplify the flow of energy, promot balance and emotional release.

- Energy feels sluggish, and procrastination becomes a pattern.

Reiki for the Solar Plexus can help **soften internal tension,** **release held anger,** and restore **inner clarity and confidence.** Hand placements over the upper abdomen, combined with deep breathing and supportive affirmations, allow this chakra to realign with its natural rhythm of **empowered movement.**

A balanced Solar Plexus, supported by the Wood Element, says:

"I know what I want. I trust myself to pursue it."

As a practitioner, when you focus Reiki energy here, you are doing more than easing physical symptoms—you are helping a person **remember their direction.**

Emotion: Anger – The Energy of Movement and Boundaries

Anger is often misunderstood—rejected, repressed, or feared. But in the wisdom of the **Wood Element**, **anger is not destructive by nature**. It is directional. It arises when something important has been blocked, crossed, or suppressed. It is a **messenger**, signaling where growth has been stifled, where boundaries have been ignored, or where truth is begging to be expressed.

In balance, anger gives us:

- Clarity about what matters
- The courage to act
- The strength to protect ourselves and others
- The motivation to create change

When Wood energy is **stuck**, anger simmers below the surface. It may show up as:

- Irritability or passive aggression
- Muscle tension or grinding teeth
- Chronic resentment or frustration
- Sudden outbursts that feel disproportionate

When Wood energy is **deficient**, anger becomes suppressed:

- You may feel like you "can't speak up" or "don't know what you want"
- You agree to things that don't align with your truth

Conscious breathwork and focused mantras help direct and amplify the flow of energy, promote balance and emotional release.

- You feel emotionally numb or lost in cycles of indecision

Through Reiki, anger is not judged—it is **invited to move**.

When your hands rest gently on the Solar Plexus, Liver area, or along the gallbladder meridian, you're not just easing physical tension—you're giving space for that emotion to speak, be seen, and shift. With Reiki, anger transforms into **assertiveness, direction**, and **clear action**.

It says:

"I have outgrown this."
"I deserve to be heard."
"I am ready to move forward."

By holding space for anger with compassion, you allow it to become what it was always meant to be—not destruction, but **growth**.

Reiki Practice for Releasing Tension and Clarifying Direction

Restoring the Flow of Movement and Choice

When the Wood Element is out of balance, it often feels like **pressurized energy**—tight muscles, pent-up emotion, mental overwhelm, or internal chaos that comes from trying to move forward without a clear path. Whether the energy is **stuck, scattered**, or **overriding your sense of ease**, Reiki can help gently release the tension and reestablish direction.

This practice is designed to soothe **Liver/Gallbladder energy**, support the **Solar Plexus**, and bring clarity to the mind and body—without forcing a decision. It works especially well during times of indecision, frustration, creative blockages, or when you're navigating life transitions.

Preparation

- Set up a quiet space with a journal nearby (for post-session clarity).
- Optional: diffuse **rosemary or peppermint essential oil**, or place a piece of **green aventurine or tiger's eye** nearby to enhance Wood energy.
- Set an intention like:
  "I allow tension to soften. My path is becoming clear."

Conscious breathwork and focused mantras help direct and amplify the flow of energy, promote balance and emotional release.

Step-by-Step Reiki Flow

1. **Begin at the Feet (Grounding for Growth)**
   Place both hands on the tops or soles of your feet.
   Imagine roots extending into the Earth. Breathe into
   this grounded support system.
   Affirm: *"I am safe to move forward."*

2. **Move to the Solar Plexus (Empowerment & Clarity)**
   Place your hands gently over your upper abdomen.
   Let your breath expand and contract naturally.
   Visualize golden-yellow light radiating outward like
   sunlight through trees.
   Affirm: *"I trust my inner guidance. I choose with
   clarity."*

3. **Liver/Gallbladder Focus (Side of Ribcage or Shoulders)**
   Place one hand over the **right side of the ribcage** (Liver
   area) and the other on the **left shoulder or side of the
   head** (Gallbladder meridian).
   Let the energy flow with your breath. If tension arises,
   exhale gently and imagine releasing it into the Earth.
   Affirm: *"I release frustration. I am ready to grow."*

4. **Third Eye Activation (Visioning)**
   Place both hands gently over your forehead or hover
   slightly above.
   Invite intuitive insight, not with force—but with trust.
   Affirm: *"My next step will become clear in the right
   time."*

Integration

After the session, remain in stillness for a few minutes. When you feel ready, journal anything that arose—emotions, images, physical sensations, or intuitive thoughts. Even if no decision becomes immediately clear, notice what **feels different**: Is the tension softer? Is your breath deeper? Has something inside you shifted?

When anger is softened and clarity begins to emerge, you don't just make decisions—you **own them**. You move forward with direction **rooted in your truth**.

Wood Element Affiramtions

(Spring | Liver & Gallbladder | Solar Plexus | Emotion: Anger)

1. *I grow with purpose and direction.*
2. *I release frustration and make space for forward movement.*
3. *I am flexible and resilient like the trees in the wind.*
4. *My path is clear, and I have the courage to walk it.*
5. *I honor my anger as a messenger, not a master.*

Conscious breathwork and focused mantras help direct and amplify the flow of energy, promote balance and emotional release.

Chapter 6: Fire Element – Passion, Joy & Heart Wisdom

Season: Summer – The Peak of Light and Expression

Summer arrives like a celebration—sunlight stretching long into the evening, flowers in full bloom, laughter spilling into the air. This is the **season of the Fire Element**, when energy rises to its peak, and life expresses itself in its most vibrant, open form.

Just as nature bursts forth in color, heat, and vitality, so too does our **inner fire**. Summer is the time of **joy, connection, intimacy, and heart-centered living**. It is the season of outward expansion, warmth in relationships, and shared experiences. The heart longs to **give, receive**, and **connect**.

In Traditional Chinese Medicine, summer's energy is described as **yang at its fullest**—active, expressive, and radiant. And yet, when this energy becomes too intense or misdirected, it can lead to **overstimulation, emotional burnout**, or the inability to fully rest. Like a fire without a hearth, our energy can scatter, leaving us exhausted, anxious, or emotionally frayed.

This is the paradox of Fire: it both **illuminates and consumes**. It must be tended with care.

In Reiki practice, aligning with Summer's energy means working with lightness, warmth, and emotional presence—while also helping to soothe and contain excess. During this season, clients may present with:

- Heart palpitations or restlessness
- Anxiety, insomnia, or hyperactivity
- Emotional highs and lows
- Difficulty maintaining emotional boundaries or feeling overly exposed

Fire needs **space to dance**, but also **structure to be safe**. Reiki offers both.

As you move through this chapter, you'll explore how to channel Reiki energy in a way that supports the **Heart's wisdom**, cools emotional overdrive, and reignites joy from within—not as a performance, but as a **natural state of being**.

"In the light of summer, I allow myself to be seen, to feel, to love—and to rest."

Conscious breathwork and focused mantras help direct and amplify the flow of energy, promo balance and emotional release.

Organs: Heart & Small Intestine – The Wisdom of Emotional Truth

In the Five Element system, the **Heart** is called the "Emperor" of the body—**the ruler of emotions, consciousness, and spirit**. It is not simply a physical organ pumping blood—it is the seat of **Shen**, the spirit that governs clarity, presence, and joy.

The **Heart** allows us to feel deeply, love openly, and experience life with authenticity. When in balance, we radiate warmth, emotional intelligence, and the ability to connect with others from a space of compassion and confidence.

The **Small Intestine**, its yang partner, serves as the **discerner**— helping us **separate the pure from the impure**, not only in digestion but in thought, emotion, and experience. It plays a subtle but powerful role in emotional clarity, helping us **decide what to keep and what to release**.

When Fire energy is **excessive**, you may experience:

- Restlessness or racing thoughts
- Insomnia or trouble settling down at night
- Overstimulation (emotionally or socially)
- Mood swings, emotional reactivity, or even mania
- Heart palpitations or irregular rhythms

When Fire energy is **deficient**, symptoms may include:

- Emotional numbness or disconnection
- Social withdrawal or fear of intimacy

- A flat, joyless mood
- Coldness in the chest or extremities
- Difficulty expressing feelings or knowing what brings you joy

Reiki offers a powerful and gentle way to support both the Heart and Small Intestine—by **clearing emotional noise** and returning the spirit to its natural resting state. Hand placements over the chest, shoulders, and solar plexus can help soften mental overload, regulate emotional flow, and reconnect the client to their **true emotional frequency**: joy.

When the Heart and Small Intestine are balanced, we feel **emotionally clear, connected to purpose**, and **safe in love**—not from others, but from within.

"I trust my feelings. I trust what I hold. I trust what I release."

Conscious breathwork and focused mantras help direct and amplify the flow of energy, promote balance and emotional release.

Chakra: Heart – The Center of Compassion and Connection

At the center of your energetic body lies the **Heart Chakra**, or **Anahata**—the bridge between the physical and the spiritual, between grounding and expansion, between self and others. It is here that love, compassion, and connection are felt most deeply. And it is here that the **Fire Element shines brightest**.

The Heart Chakra governs:

- Emotional openness and intimacy
- Joy, laughter, and lightness
- Compassion for self and others
- Forgiveness and empathy
- The ability to both give and receive love

When Fire energy is in harmony, the Heart Chakra feels expansive yet calm. There is a **warmth**, a presence, a radiance that draws others in—not to seek attention, but to **share connection**. You feel safe in your vulnerability. You are able to express emotions with ease and grace.

But when Fire is **overactive**, the Heart Chakra may become:

- Scattered or overly emotional
- Prone to dramatic highs and lows
- Exhausted from giving too much or lacking emotional boundaries
- Restless, anxious, or prone to insomnia

When Fire is **deficient**, you may feel:

- Numb, emotionally closed off, or indifferent
- Unable to connect with others or feel joy
- Lonely, guarded, or unwilling to trust
- Spiritually disconnected or flat

Reiki applied to the Heart Chakra helps regulate this inner fire—**cooling it when it's overheated, and reigniting it when it's dimmed**. Your hands become like sacred hearth-keepers, tending the flame within with gentleness and care.

During Heart-focused Reiki, it is helpful to:

- Use **light touch or hovering hands** over the chest
- Invite the breath to expand gently with each inhale
- Visualize **green or soft pink light** radiating outward in a gentle wave
- Encourage the release of old emotional wounds or patterns with loving intention

A balanced Heart Chakra supported by the Fire Element says:

"I allow myself to love, to feel, and to shine—without burning out."

In the next section, we'll explore how **joy—and its distortion, mania—reveals the state of your Fire Element**, and how Reiki can gently restore equilibrium in both the emotional and energetic body.

Conscious breathwork and focused mantras help direct and amplify the flow of energy, promote balance and emotional release.

Emotion: Joy (and Mania) – The Flame of the Heart

Joy is the natural expression of the Fire Element. It's not forced or performative—it arises from a deep sense of being **alive, connected, and in alignment**. True joy doesn't need to be loud. It can be a quiet smile, a moment of gratitude, a warm breeze across your skin. It is the **heartbeat of the soul** saying, "Yes. This is it."

In the Five Element system, joy is associated with the **Heart** and its capacity to hold **Shen**—the spirit. When Shen is calm and present, joy flows. When Shen is disturbed or scattered, joy becomes distorted into **mania**—a kind of frantic, unstable energy that may seem happy on the surface but is actually rooted in overstimulation, anxiety, or emotional depletion.

When Fire is Balanced (Joy):

- You feel emotionally available and present.
- You experience authentic laughter, warmth, and intimacy.
- You connect with others easily, but maintain healthy emotional boundaries.
- You are able to rest and play without guilt.
- You move through life with lightness and ease.

When Fire is Excessive (Mania):

- You may feel hyperactive, giddy, or overly reactive.

- You struggle with **emotional regulation**, bouncing between highs and lows.
- You may have **difficulty sleeping** or feel "wired but tired."
- You chase stimulation to avoid stillness.
- Emotionally, you may become overly dependent on others for validation.

When Fire is Deficient (Emotional Numbness):

- Joy feels unreachable or fake.
- You withdraw emotionally or spiritually.
- There's a lack of connection—both within and with others.
- You may feel flat, uninspired, or spiritually adrift.

Reiki offers a sacred space where **excess energy can settle** and **dormant joy can reawaken**. By focusing on the **Heart Chakra** and the **Fire element pathways**, you help the client return to a state of emotional equilibrium—not too much, not too little. Just enough.

It's not about making someone "happy"—it's about helping them feel **safe enough to feel again**.

A heart in balance says:

"I allow joy to rise in its own time. I am not afraid to feel."

And from that space of still, steady fire—**light begins to return**.

Conscious breathwork and focused mantras help direct and amplify the flow of energy, promo balance and emotional release.

Reiki Practice to Balance Hyperactivity and Emotional Burnout

Soothing the Fire, Reigniting the Soul

When the Fire Element is unbalanced, the system often swings between two extremes: **emotional overload** and **complete emotional withdrawal**. One moment there's overstimulation, racing thoughts, and restlessness; the next, exhaustion, numbness, or burnout. In both cases, the Shen—the spirit of the heart—struggles to find peace.

This Reiki practice supports the **Heart and Small Intestine meridians**, the **Heart Chakra**, and the emotional rhythms of the Fire Element. It is especially helpful when your client (or you) feels emotionally frayed, overwhelmed, hypersensitive, or disconnected from joy.

Preparation

- Create a calming space with **soft pink or green tones**, gentle lighting, and quiet music.
- Diffuse calming Fire-balancing oils like **lavender, rose, or sandalwood**.
- Invite stillness. Set the intention:
  "I allow my heart to rest. I return to the center of joy."

Step-by-Step Reiki Flow

1. **Begin at the Heart**
   Place your hands lightly on the **center of the chest**, or hover just above.
   Focus only on breath—nothing else.
   Inhale slowly through the nose, exhale gently through the mouth.
   Visualize **soft pink or emerald green light** expanding with each breath.
   Affirm: *"I am safe to soften. My spirit is at peace."*

2. **Move to the Head (Cooling the Mind)**
   Place your hands gently over the **forehead or temples**, or rest them on either side of the head.
   Imagine **heat dissipating**, like steam rising from warm earth after a summer rain.
   Affirm: *"My thoughts are light. My energy is calm."*

3. **Small Intestine Meridian Support (Discernment)**
   Optional: Hold the **outer edge of the hand (karate chop area)** or trace down from the **shoulder to the pinky finger** to gently stimulate the Small Intestine channel.
   Invite clarity: *"I keep what nourishes me. I release what does not."*

4. **Finish at the Knees or Feet (Grounding the Fire)**
   Bring your hands to the **knees or soles of the feet** to complete the circuit and anchor the energy.
   Let the warmth move **down and out**, grounding excess Fire.
   Affirm: *"My heart is light. My body is calm. I rest in joy."*

Conscious breathwork and focused mantras help direct and amplify the flow of energy, promoting balance and emotional release.

Integration

After the session, encourage reflection or stillness rather than immediate action. Suggest drinking cool or room-temperature herbal tea (such as **hibiscus** or **lemon balm**) and resting in nature if possible.

When Fire is balanced, the heart beats steadily, emotions move freely, and **joy returns without effort**. The body no longer chases stimulation to feel alive—it simply **remembers how to be**..

Fire Element Affirmations

(Summer | Heart & Small Intestine | Heart | Emotion: Joy/Mania)

1. *I radiate joy from the center of my being.*
2. *My heart is open, and my spirit is calm.*
3. *I am allowed to rest, even in the light.*
4. *I give and receive love freely and without fear.*
5. *I am safe to feel, to laugh, and to shine.*

Chapter 7: Earth Element – Nurturing, Stability & Worry

Season: Late Summer – The Pause Between Becoming and Letting Go

Late Summer is the **season of stillness**, when the heat of summer softens and the first golden hints of autumn begin to whisper through the trees. It is the **space between**—after the height of expression (Fire) and before the release (Metal). It's a time of reflection, integration, and **digestion**, not just of food, but of experiences, emotions, and ideas.

This is the time of the **Earth Element**—the center of the elemental cycle. Earth is the ground beneath your feet and the gravity that holds you steady. It nourishes, protects, and connects. It is the **home within yourself**.

In Traditional Chinese Medicine, Earth energy represents **support, nourishment, and emotional stability**. It is the season of **harvest**—not just gathering what has grown, but also deciding what will sustain you going forward.

During Late Summer, we are invited to:

Conscious breathwork and focused mantras help direct and amplify the flow of energy, promote balance and emotional release.

- Slow down
- Digest what we've experienced
- Center ourselves
- Reconnect to routine, rhythm, and simplicity
- Reflect on what truly nourishes our body, mind, and soul

In Reiki practice, this season often brings clients who feel **scattered, overextended, or disconnected from their center**. Many are caring for others while neglecting themselves. Others are mentally overloaded or feeling stuck in cycles of worry or overthinking.

When you align with Earth energy, your Reiki sessions become **an offering of grounding, nourishment, and presence**—helping clients return to a state of **emotional and energetic equilibrium**.

"I return to the center. I am held. I am enough."

Organs: Spleen & Stomach – Digestion of Life

The **Spleen and Stomach** are the key organs associated with the Earth Element. In Traditional Chinese Medicine, their function goes far beyond physical digestion—they are responsible for how we **process, assimilate, and integrate** not only food, but **thoughts, experiences, and emotions**.

The **Stomach** receives nourishment—both literal and energetic. It is the container, the first place of intake. The **Spleen**, its yin counterpart, transforms and distributes that nourishment throughout the body and mind, giving us clarity, energy, and emotional steadiness.

Together, they represent the ability to:

- Feel supported
- Maintain boundaries while caring for others
- Think clearly without becoming overwhelmed
- Be emotionally centered and resilient
- Ground and digest new experiences with ease

When Earth energy is **imbalanced**, it often shows up through these organs.

Excessive Earth (Overextension or Co-dependency):

- Over-giving or difficulty saying no
- Obsessive thinking or worry
- Overeating or emotional eating
- Feeling heavy, bloated, or sluggish

Conscious breathwork and focused mantras help direct and amplify the flow of energy, promote balance and emotional release.

- Craving sweets or carbohydrates
- Mental fog or lack of clarity

Deficient Earth (Lack of Support or Nourishment):

- Fatigue or weak digestion
- Poor appetite or trouble focusing
- Feeling ungrounded or scattered
- Emotional instability or feeling unsupported
- Difficulty concentrating or finishing tasks

Reiki over the **abdomen and solar plexus** can be deeply comforting and restorative. A slow, steady session helps the client feel **safe, seen,** and **held**—allowing them to drop into a sense of **inner quiet and trust.** Placing hands over the **midsection** not only supports the digestive organs physically, but it also helps energetically **"digest life"**—clearing mental and emotional clutter.

The Spleen and Stomach thrive with simplicity, warmth, and rhythm. Reiki honors this by offering **nourishment without effort**—a quiet return to center.

"I receive. I process. I am supported by life."

Chakras: Solar Plexus & Root – The Ground of Identity and Belonging

The Earth Element is supported by two powerful energy centers: the **Solar Plexus** and the **Root Chakra**. Together, they form a stable foundation for personal power, self-trust, and emotional security. When these chakras are balanced, you feel **centered, calm, capable, and connected**—able to nourish others without losing yourself in the process.

Solar Plexus Chakra – Your Inner Support System

The **Solar Plexus** governs personal identity, confidence, and self-worth. In the context of the Earth Element, it also represents your **ability to process life**—to take in experiences, evaluate them, and determine your response.

When Earth energy is imbalanced here, you may:

- Overanalyze situations or obsess over small details
- Feel uncertain about your direction or purpose
- Seek external validation or approval to feel secure
- Struggle with digestion or fatigue in the core

Reiki at the Solar Plexus helps to **clear mental clutter, soothe nervous overactivity**, and restore the client's sense of personal power. The energy here should feel warm, steady, and deeply anchoring.

Root Chakra – Your Connection to the Ground Beneath You

Conscious breathwork and focused mantras help direct and amplify the flow of energy, promote balance and emotional release.

The **Root Chakra** governs your sense of safety, stability, and belonging. It reflects your relationship to the physical world—home, money, family, and body—and gives you the feeling that you are **safe to exist**, just as you are.

When Earth is imbalanced at the Root Chakra, you may:

- Feel unsupported or chronically anxious
- Over-give in relationships to feel secure
- Struggle with grounding or staying present
- Experience lower-body tension or fatigue

Reiki over the Root Chakra helps restore a deep sense of **embodiment and connection to the Earth**. It reminds the client that they are **held, worthy, and enough**, even when they're not doing anything at all.

By working with these two chakras, you help clients move from **worry to trust**, from **scattered energy to grounded strength**, and from **mental overactivity to emotional steadiness**.

A balanced Earth energy within the chakras whispers:

"You are supported. You are centered. You are whole."

Emotion: Worry & Overthinking – When the Mind Tries to Nurture the Soul

The emotion most closely linked to the **Earth Element** is **worry**—especially the kind that loops endlessly in the mind, attempting to fix, control, or anticipate every outcome. Worry is a form of misplaced caretaking. It wants to help, to solve, to keep everyone (including yourself) safe. But in excess, it becomes heavy, exhausting, and disempowering.

Unlike the sharp flash of fear or the fiery burst of anger, worry is **slow and sticky**. It settles in like fog, clouding clarity and weighing down the spirit. Left unchecked, it leads to:

- Indecision and second-guessing
- Mental fatigue and brain fog
- Nervous stomach, digestive upset, or nausea
- Emotional co-dependency ("If they're not okay, I can't be okay.")
- Difficulty receiving support or letting go of control

Worry often stems from a **lack of inner nourishment**. When the Earth Element is depleted, we look to the outside world to ground us—seeking reassurance, routine, or control. But the healing lies in **returning to center**, not seeking more stimulation or solutions.

How Reiki Supports Worry

Conscious breathwork and focused mantras help direct and amplify the flow of energy, promot. balance and emotional release.

Reiki gently soothes the mental and emotional "buzz" of worry by inviting stillness, presence, and reconnection to the body. It doesn't try to quiet the mind by force—it **softens the edges** of thought until the heart can be heard again.

During Reiki:

- Place hands over the **Solar Plexus** or **forehead** to calm looping thoughts.
- Anchor the session at the **Root Chakra** to restore a sense of security and grounding.
- Allow energy to settle like soil after a heavy rain— slow, heavy, and peaceful.

You may notice clients sigh, feel their stomach gurgle (a good sign of nervous system reset), or say things like, *"My mind feels clear for the first time in days."*

The goal isn't to stop thinking. It's to return thought to its natural rhythm—**gentle, grounded, and guided by trust.**

A balanced Earth Element brings this realization:

"I don't have to think my way to safety. I already am safe."

Reiki Practice for Grounding, Digestion, and Inner Peace

Returning to the Center Within

The Earth Element thrives on stability, rhythm, and nourishment—not just from food, but from emotional safety, mental clarity, and meaningful connection. When Earth energy is imbalanced, Reiki becomes a powerful tool to help **rebuild the foundation, soothe the nervous system**, and support the body's ability to **digest life** again—physically, mentally, and emotionally.

This session is especially helpful for clients experiencing overthinking, digestive discomfort, emotional burnout from caregiving, or feeling "unmoored" after a major transition.

Preparation

- Set the tone with earthy colors (yellows, browns, soft greens) and warm lighting.
- Optional tools: place a **smoky quartz or tiger's eye** near the Root, and diffuse **ginger or sweet orange oil** to support digestion and emotional grounding.
- Set a gentle intention:
  "I am safe. I am nourished. I am home in myself."

Conscious breathwork and focused mantras help direct and amplify the flow of energy, promo balance and emotional release.

Step-by-Step Reiki Flow

1. **Begin at the Feet (Anchoring Earth Energy)**
   Place your hands gently on or just above the **soles of the feet**.
   Visualize roots growing deep into the Earth, drawing up warm, golden light.
   Affirm: *"I am grounded. I am connected to the Earth."*

2. **Move to the Root Chakra (Stability)**
   Bring your hands to the **base of the spine or lower abdomen**.
   Imagine a rich, earthy red light spinning slowly, calmly.
   Let the energy settle. Let the body feel safe.
   Affirm: *"I am safe. I belong. I trust the rhythm of life."*

3. **Solar Plexus & Stomach (Digesting Thought and Emotion)**
   Place both hands over the **upper abdomen**.
   Feel warmth building here like the gentle sun of late summer.
   If the client is open to it, encourage slow breathing into the belly.
   Affirm: *"I process with ease. I absorb what serves me. I let the rest go."*

4. **Optional: Third Eye or Shoulders (Releasing Mental Clutter)**
   To clear looping thoughts, place your hands lightly on the **forehead** or over the **shoulders**.
   Encourage energy to move down and out of the head.
   Affirm: *"My thoughts are soft. I rest in clarity."*

5. **Close with Integration at the Heart or Feet**
   Return to the **Heart Chakra** for warmth and self-compassion, or the **feet** for deep grounding.

Let stillness complete the session. Allow the body to fully receive.

Post-Session Suggestions

After the session, offer grounding foods (warm tea, a light snack), gentle movement (walking in nature), or journaling with a prompt like:
"What truly nourishes me?"

This is not a time to leap forward. Earth teaches us to **pause, receive, and trust the strength of simplicity**. Reiki, in this space, becomes not just a healing technique—but a form of **energetic nourishment**.

"In stillness, I find peace. In the center, I remember who I am."

Earth Element Affirmations

(Late Summer | Spleen & Stomach | Solar Plexus & Root | Emotion: Worry/Overthinking)

1. *I am grounded, nourished, and supported by life.*
2. *I release the need to overthink—I trust the present moment.*
3. *I digest experiences with ease and grace.*
4. *I give to others without losing myself.*
5. *I am enough, exactly as I am.*

Conscious breathwork and focused mantras help direct and amplify the flow of energy, promote balance and emotional release.

Chapter 8: Metal Element – Clarity, Grief & Letting Go

Season: Autumn – The Sacred Art of Release

Autumn arrives like an exhale—a soft surrender after the intensity of summer. The air cools, the leaves turn, and nature begins the sacred process of **letting go**. Trees drop their leaves not out of failure, but out of wisdom. They know the beauty of release. They understand the strength it takes to **simplify, strip back, and prepare for renewal**.

This is the season of the **Metal Element**, the energy of **refinement, reflection, and clarity**. It teaches us to discern what is essential and what must be released. It asks us to look within, honor what we've outgrown, and find the **preciousness in what remains**.

Metal energy invites you to:

- Breathe deeply and consciously
- Let go of emotional and energetic waste
- Reconnect to your inner wisdom
- Honor your grief without being consumed by it

- Embrace the beauty of minimalism—energetically, emotionally, and spiritually

In Reiki practice, Autumn often brings clients who are feeling **emotionally heavy, energetically cluttered, or spiritually disconnected**. They may be grieving losses, navigating transitions, or feeling called to release what no longer serves—but unsure how.

By aligning your sessions with the energy of Autumn, you create space for your clients to **exhale**—to release with grace, and to rediscover the clear, shining truth at the center of their being.

"I breathe in clarity. I release with love. I am free to begin again."

Conscious breathwork and focused mantras help direct and amplify the flow of energy, promot balance and emotional release.

Organs: Lungs & Large Intestine – The Breath of Life and the Power of Release

In Traditional Chinese Medicine, the **Lungs and Large Intestine** are the paired organs of the **Metal Element**. Together, they govern our ability to take in what is pure, let go of what is not, and maintain a sense of **energetic and emotional boundaries**.

The Lungs – Sacred Breath, Sacred Presence

The **Lungs** are the first organs to interact with the world. With every inhale, they draw in not just oxygen, but **life force (Qi)**. They represent our ability to **receive**—to welcome in inspiration, beauty, connection, and presence. Spiritually, the Lungs are said to house the **Po**, the corporeal soul that connects us to the physical body and the material world.

When Lung energy is strong, we:

- Feel emotionally open but protected
- Communicate clearly and with compassion
- Breathe fully and freely
- Feel inspired and connected to Spirit

When the Lungs are imbalanced, we may experience:

- Shallow breathing or breath-holding
- Sadness, melancholy, or deep unresolved grief
- Skin issues (the Lungs govern the skin)
- A sense of heaviness in the chest
- Withdrawal or hypersensitivity to others

The Large Intestine – The Wisdom of Letting Go

The **Large Intestine** is the final stage of digestion—responsible for the **elimination of waste**. On an energetic level, it helps us determine what thoughts, emotions, patterns, or relationships we need to **release** in order to stay in balance. It asks:

"What are you still holding onto that no longer serves you?"

When Large Intestine energy is healthy, we:

- Let go of the past with ease
- Maintain energetic clarity and boundaries
- Feel emotionally lighter and more focused
- Trust our body's natural rhythms

When imbalanced, we may struggle with:

- Constipation or elimination issues
- Resistance to change or fear of release
- Rigid thinking or perfectionism
- Emotional stagnation or grief that feels "stuck"

In Reiki sessions, working over the **chest, throat, and lower abdomen** can support the energetic flow of these organs. Your hands offer clients the permission they may not have given themselves:
To breathe deeply. To feel fully. To let go gently.

"I take in what uplifts me. I release what weighs me down. I honor the space in between."

Chakras: Throat & Third Eye – Expression and Insight in the Space of Stillness

The Metal Element resonates strongly with the upper chakras—especially the **Throat** and **Third Eye**—where breath becomes voice, and experience becomes wisdom. These chakras offer us the tools to **express our truth, grieve with grace**, and **see clearly** through the fog of emotional clutter.

Throat Chakra – Vishuddha

The **Throat Chakra** governs **communication, truth, and expression**. In the Metal Element, this center reflects our ability to **breathe through emotion, speak what needs to be said**, and **honor silence** when words are not enough.

When balanced, the Throat Chakra allows us to:

- Express grief without shame
- Speak clearly and calmly
- Set healthy boundaries
- Know when to communicate—and when to listen

When imbalanced through Metal disharmony, you may experience:

- A "lump in the throat" sensation
- Sore throat, cough, or voice strain
- Withholding emotions out of fear of burdening others

- Difficulty saying goodbye or asking for what you need

Reiki at the throat is incredibly soothing for those holding back unspoken emotion. Even a light hovering hand here, paired with breath-focused Reiki, can release years of stored sorrow.

Third Eye Chakra – Ajna

The **Third Eye Chakra** is the seat of **inner vision, insight, and spiritual clarity**. In the Metal Element, it invites you to **discern what is essential**, to release distraction, and to focus on what truly matters. This chakra supports the refinement that Metal demands—the sifting of truth from illusion.

When balanced, the Third Eye helps you:

- See your grief as part of your transformation
- Perceive meaning beyond the moment
- Make space for inner guidance
- Let go of attachments with clarity and grace

When out of balance with Metal energy, you may:

- Feel mentally cluttered or foggy
- Obsess over the past or resist closure
- Struggle to access intuition
- Avoid spiritual stillness or quiet reflection

Reiki to the Third Eye during a Metal-aligned session helps bring peace to the mind and insight to the heart. It clears the lens through which we view our past, allowing forgiveness, perspective, and transformation to unfold naturally.

Conscious breathwork and focused mantras help direct and amplify the flow of energy, promote balance and emotional release.

By supporting the **Throat and Third Eye Chakras** together, Reiki becomes a tool of both **release and revelation**. You help your client express grief, find peace in the pause, and reconnect with the beauty of letting go.

"I speak my truth. I see with clarity. I let go with love."

Emotion: Grief – The Sacred Weight of What Was Loved

Grief is not a weakness. It is not something to be rushed, bypassed, or "healed away." In the wisdom of the **Metal Element**, grief is a sacred process—an act of honoring what has been lost, changed, or completed. It is the **emotional alchemy** that transforms attachment into memory, pain into wisdom, and endings into clarity.

Grief shows us what mattered.
It speaks to the depth of our love.
It reminds us that we are human—tender, porous, and beautifully alive.

The Nature of Grief in the Metal Element

Grief, when allowed to move, is like the autumn wind: cool, cleansing, and eventually still. But when it becomes stuck—unexpressed or held too tightly—it weighs us down like wet leaves, making the breath shallow, the voice tight, and the heart heavy.

Imbalanced Metal energy expresses grief in many ways:

- A chronic sense of loss, even when nothing specific has been lost
- Shallow or strained breathing
- A tendency to withdraw or isolate emotionally
- Perfectionism or hyper-control as a way to avoid feeling

Conscious breathwork and focused mantras help direct and amplify the flow of energy, promot balance and emotional release.

- Difficulty letting go—of people, emotions, or physical objects

When balanced, grief becomes what it was always meant to be: a bridge between the past and the present. It no longer consumes—but completes. It brings **beauty, reverence, and a deeper connection to the soul**.

How Reiki Supports Grief

Reiki offers what grief often needs most: **gentle presence**.

It doesn't push. It doesn't fix. It **holds space for the emotion to breathe**, soften, and move—at its own pace. By focusing on the **lungs, throat, heart, and Third Eye**, Reiki allows clients to feel without being overwhelmed, and to begin the sacred process of release.

Clients may cry, sigh, or feel a lightness they can't quite explain. That is the energy of grief shifting. Not disappearing—but evolving.

"I honor what I've lost. I keep what remains. I release what no longer belongs."

Reiki, paired with the Metal Element, becomes a quiet ceremony—one that invites stillness, dignity, and clarity to enter the healing space.

Reiki Practice to Support Breath, Release, and Clarity

Creating Space for What Wants to Be Let Go

When the **Metal Element** is imbalanced—through unresolved grief, emotional stagnation, or mental overwhelm—Reiki offers a quiet invitation back to the breath, back to presence, and back to the clarity that comes only after release.

This session is ideal during times of mourning, transition, emotional heaviness, or spiritual fatigue. It allows clients to **exhale fully**, not just through the lungs, but through the entire energetic body.

Preparation

- Keep the space **minimal and calm**—cool colors, soft lighting, and silence or slow instrumental music.
- Optional: Diffuse **eucalyptus or frankincense**, or offer a **white feather or clear quartz** nearby to symbolize purification and air.
- Set an intention like:
  "I create space to breathe. I honor what was. I receive what is next."

Conscious breathwork and focused mantras help direct and amplify the flow of energy, promoting balance and emotional release.

Step-by-Step Reiki Flow

1. **Start at the Lungs (Sacred Breath)**
   Place your hands gently over the **chest**, just beneath the collarbones.
   Invite the client to take slow, conscious breaths.
   As they inhale, visualize cool, white light filling the lungs.
   As they exhale, visualize heaviness being released into the Earth.
   Affirm: *"I breathe in peace. I exhale what I no longer need."*

2. **Throat Chakra (Expression & Softening)**
   Move to the **throat area**, using either a hovering hand or a light, still touch.
   Allow any emotions that rise to be felt without judgment.
   If tears come, hold steady. The release is the Reiki.
   Affirm: *"I give voice to my truth. I let it move through me."*

3. **Lower Abdomen (Supporting Letting Go)**
   Place hands over the **lower belly**, supporting the energy of the **Large Intestine**.
   Invite the body to release physically, emotionally, energetically.
   This is the "final sweep" of old energy. Let it be soft.
   Affirm: *"I let go with love. I trust the space that remains."*

4. **Third Eye (Clarity and Visioning)**
   Finish by gently placing your hands over the **forehead**.
   Invite the client to envision what life could feel like with more space, more clarity.
   Breathe together. Invite stillness.

Affirm: *"I see clearly. I accept this moment with grace."*

Integration

After the session, suggest a simple ritual of closure—a walk in nature, journaling a goodbye letter (even if never sent), or sitting with a candle in silence.

Grief doesn't always end. But it evolves. And with Reiki, it can move—like air through trees, like leaves falling to make room for new life.

"With each breath, I return to myself. I let go with gratitude. I begin again."

Metal Element Affirmations

(Autumn | Lungs & Large Intestine | Throat & Third Eye | Emotion: Grief)

1. *I breathe in clarity and exhale all that I no longer need.*
2. *I honor what has passed, and I release it with love.*
3. *I speak my truth and live with integrity.*
4. *In letting go, I create space for what is sacred.*
5. *I trust the beauty of simplicity and the wisdom of stillness.*

Conscious breathwork and focused mantras help direct and amplify the flow of energy, promote balance and emotional release.

PART 3:
DEEPENING THE
PRACTICE

Chapter 9: Creating Elemental Reiki Sessions

How to Assess Element Imbalances in Clients

Reading Energy Through the Lens of Nature

As a Reiki practitioner working with the Five Elements, your role expands beyond simply channeling energy—you become a **translator of nature's language within the body**. Assessing which element is out of balance in your client offers powerful insight into the root of their emotional, physical, and energetic challenges.

Each person holds all Five Elements within them, but depending on life circumstances, personality traits, and stressors, one or more elements may become **excessive, deficient, or stagnant**. Identifying this pattern allows you to create a session that is **deeply personalized**, not just symptom-based.

The Energy of Excess vs. Deficiency

- **Excess Elemental Energy** often feels **loud, hot,** or **tight** in the field. You might sense restlessness, irritation, swelling, or emotional overwhelm.

Just for today, I will let go of worry and trust the flow of life.

- **Deficient Elemental Energy** feels **quiet, dull,** or **collapsed**. It may show up as fatigue, indecision, disconnection, or emotional flatness.

Both types of imbalance are asking for **realignment**, not judgment. Through Reiki, your hands become the listening device—and the harmonizer.

Three Core Questions to Ask Before a Session:

1. **Which element is most present in the client's current experience?**
   (Are they fiery and scattered, watery and fearful, earthy and stuck in overthinking?)
2. **What is the emotional tone beneath the symptoms?**
   (Is it grief, anger, worry, fear, or a loss of joy?)
3. **What season or life phase are they currently in or resisting?**
   (Are they trying to grow but feel stuck? Letting go? Being called inward?)

These questions, combined with subtle energetic cues, help you form a clear understanding of where your client needs support.

In the next section, we'll explore practical tools you can use—like **muscle testing, facial diagnosis, and emotional pulse awareness**—to deepen your understanding of elemental imbalances and enhance your Reiki assessments.

"To assess is to listen. And in the listening, healing begins."

Tools: Muscle Testing, Facial Diagnosis & Emotional Pulse Awareness

Tuning into the Subtle Messages of the Body

While your intuition and Reiki hands are powerful guides, there are also time-tested tools from Traditional Chinese Medicine, kinesiology, and energy medicine that can help you assess **elemental imbalances** with more clarity and confidence. These techniques are gentle, accessible, and easily woven into any Reiki session.

Muscle Testing (Applied Kinesiology)

Accessing the Body's Inner Compass

Muscle testing, also known as **Applied Kinesiology**, is a powerful tool that allows practitioners to tap into the body's **innate intelligence**. The body "knows" what it needs—and more importantly, what it does not. Muscle testing offers a way to bypass mental chatter and receive direct, energetic feedback from the **subconscious mind and energy field**.

When used in the context of **elemental imbalances**, muscle testing can reveal whether a specific **element, organ system, chakra, or emotion** is under stress, overstimulated, or in need of support. It's especially helpful when clients feel overwhelmed or unsure of what they need, giving you a clear direction for your Reiki session.

Just for today, I will let go of worry and trust the flow of life.

Why It Works

When the body is exposed to a **truth**, a resonant frequency, or a supportive energy, the nervous system strengthens and the muscle holds firm.
When exposed to **stress, dissonance, or overload**, the system weakens momentarily—causing a temporary "drop" or weakness in the muscle being tested.

This doesn't mean something is broken—it simply means the energy around that subject is **unbalanced, blocked, or depleted**.

How to Perform a Basic Muscle Test

1. Establish a baseline:

- Have the client stand or sit upright.
- Ask them to extend one arm straight out from the shoulder, palm down.
- Place two fingers on their wrist or forearm and press down gently while they resist.
- Say, *"Say 'My name is (their name).'"* Test the strength. Then try a false name, like *"My name is Bob."* This shows them what a strong vs. weak response feels like.

2. Ask Elemental Questions or Affirmations:
Once your baseline is established, begin testing with relevant prompts. For example:

- *"Is your Water Element in balance?"*
- *"My Liver is flowing with ease."*

- *"My Fire Element is grounded and calm."*
- *"My Lungs are open to letting go."*

Observe whether the arm holds strong or gives way. A weak response often indicates an **imbalance, unresolved emotion, or energetic overload** in that area.

Ways to Customize the Test

You can go beyond verbal affirmations by **placing energetic tools in the client's field** during the test to see what strengthens or weakens their system:

- **Essential oils:** Have them hold a bottle of an oil aligned with an element (e.g., *lavender* for Fire, *cedarwood* for Earth) and test.
- **Crystals:** Place a crystal over a chakra or have them hold it (e.g., *lapis lazuli* for Metal/Throat Chakra).
- **Chakra names:** Say or visualize chakras while testing (e.g., *"Root Chakra"*) to identify energetic congestion.
- **Elemental symbols or colors:** Show cards or fabric swatches with colors tied to each element and test for resonance.

What to Do With the Results

- A **strong response** suggests the area is balanced or supported.
- A **weak response** suggests the area is imbalanced, overworked, or in need of energetic attention.

Just for today, I will let go of worry and trust the flow of life.

Use this information to:

- Choose which **Reiki hand positions** to emphasize
- Select **affirmations, oils, crystals, or sound frequencies** to incorporate
- Confirm which **elemental visualization or self-care ritual** would benefit the client post-session

Tips for Success

- Always get **clear permission** before muscle testing.
- Stay **neutral and grounded**—don't mentally "push" for a result.
- Use **gentle pressure**—this is about subtle energy, not strength.
- Have the client stay hydrated—**dehydration can distort results**.
- If in doubt, test again, or try a different method to cross-reference.

Muscle testing is not about "diagnosing," but about **listening energetically**—a way to ask the body, *"What do you need right now?"* and trust its answer. When paired with the elemental lens, it becomes a beautiful diagnostic compass for your healing sessions.

"The body never lies. It simply waits to be heard."

Facial Diagnosis – Reading the Face Like a Map

The Face Reflects the Soul's Seasons

In the wisdom of Traditional Chinese Medicine (TCM), the **face is a mirror of the inner terrain**. Long before high-tech diagnostics, practitioners observed the subtleties of facial color, lines, texture, tone, and expression to understand the state of a person's health—physically, emotionally, and energetically.

As a Reiki practitioner working with the **Five Elements**, facial diagnosis offers you a beautiful, non-invasive way to "read" where energy is flowing freely—and where it may be congested, depleted, or emotionally held.

The face reveals **more than symptoms**—it tells a story. And when viewed through the elemental lens, each area of the face reflects the balance or imbalance of a particular **organ pair and emotional state**.

How to Use Facial Diagnosis in Practice

Facial reading does not require deep medical knowledge. It begins with presence. Simply sit across from your client and **observe with compassionate curiosity**, noticing:

- **Color** and undertones of the skin
- **Texture** (dryness, puffiness, oiliness, tightness)
- **Lines** or areas of tension
- **Emotional expression** or absence thereof
- **Asymmetry** between left and right

Then gently consider which element may be showing up most prominently.

Just for today, I will let go of worry and trust the flow of life.

Key Facial Indicators by Element

Water (Kidneys & Bladder)

- **Dark circles or puffiness under the eyes**
- A **blue-gray tint** to the skin
- A withdrawn or hollow look in the eyes
- Deep, vertical lines at the inner corners of the eyes
- A fearful or cautious emotional tone

May suggest fear, exhaustion, adrenal depletion, or a need for deeper rest and support.

Wood (Liver & Gallbladder)

- **Greenish or olive tone** to the skin, especially at the temples
- **Tension in the jaw**, neck, or outer brow area
- **Vertical lines between the eyebrows** (often called the "11s")
- Eyes that look sharp, focused, or agitated
- Facial tightness or clenching

May reflect suppressed anger, frustration, or energetic stagnation—often in need of movement and release.

Fire (Heart & Small Intestine)

- **Redness or flushed cheeks**, especially when not related to temperature
- **Darting, overly bright, or unfocused eyes**
- Overly animated facial expressions or excessive laughter
- Visible blood vessels near the nose or cheeks
- Twitching, sweating, or hyperactivity

May indicate overstimulation, emotional overwhelm, or an "overheated" system in need of cooling and calming.

Earth (Spleen & Stomach)

- **Yellow undertone** to the skin, particularly around the mouth
- **Worry lines** across the forehead
- **Sagging or full cheeks**
- Puffiness or heaviness in the lower face
- Lips that are pale, dry, or cracked

Often shows up in those who are mentally overactive, emotionally overextended, or lacking grounded support.

Metal (Lungs & Large Intestine)

- **Pale, dry, or thin skin**
- **Horizontal lines on the upper forehead**
- Sadness in the eyes or a distant gaze
- A collapsed or flat facial expression
- Weak or shallow breath observable through the rise and fall of the chest

Just for today, I will let go of worry and trust the flow of life.

Points to unresolved grief, a need for release, or difficulty letting go—physically or emotionally.

Why It Matters

When you begin your Reiki session with facial diagnosis, you are already **in conversation with the energy body**—listening to what is unspoken, witnessing what longs to be acknowledged. This skill complements other tools like muscle testing, intuition, and pulse awareness, helping you refine your **elemental approach** with care.

Always view the face through a **lens of compassion**, not critique. Facial cues don't label someone as "broken" or "imbalanced"—they simply guide you toward **what wants attention, healing, and harmony**.

"The face does not hide. It reflects. And when you learn to read it with reverence, it tells you exactly where to begin."

Pulse & Emotional Awareness

Listening to the Energy Beneath the Words

You don't need to be trained in Traditional Chinese pulse diagnosis to read the **emotional pulse** of your client. You already do it intuitively—through their voice, their breath, their posture, and the way they walk into the room.

The **pulse of emotion** is subtle yet powerful. It's the frequency beneath the conversation, the energy woven between sentences. As a Reiki practitioner working with the Five Elements, tuning into this emotional rhythm allows you to assess **not just what's being said—but what's being felt, held, and hidden.**

What to Observe in the Emotional Pulse

Pay attention to how your client speaks, moves, and holds themselves—these clues often reveal **elemental imbalances** before a word is even exchanged.

Fire/Wood Imbalance

- **Fast-paced speaking**, interrupting self, jumping between thoughts
- Restlessness or pacing
- Sudden bursts of emotion—laughter, irritation, tears
- Tone of voice may be sharp, high-pitched, or rapid-fire

Just for today, I will let go of worry and trust the flow of life.

Often indicates overstimulated energy—too much yang, ungrounded enthusiasm, frustration, or emotional overwhelm.

Metal/Water Imbalance

- **Quiet voice**, long pauses, eyes turned downward or away
- Breath may be shallow, held, or skipped
- Tone may feel hollow, flat, or overly careful
- Tearfulness or emotional restraint may be felt just beneath the surface

Often points to grief, fear, emotional suppression, or deep sadness that hasn't been processed.

Earth Imbalance

- **Repetitive stories**, explaining too much, circling around a point
- Tone may sound apologetic or uncertain
- Desire to be understood or validated
- Energy may feel heavy, tired, or overly accommodating

Often reflects worry, overthinking, boundary issues, or a need for reassurance and support.

Other Signs to Notice

- **Does their voice match their energy?** Someone saying "I'm fine" in a shaky or tight tone may not be.

- **Where is their breath?** Shallow in the chest (Metal), held in the belly (Earth), or rapid (Fire)?
- **What is their posture or gaze telling you?** Upright and expansive (balanced), or collapsed and withdrawn (deficient)?

Tuning In, Not Tuning Out

This is not about **analyzing** your client—it's about attuning to their **vibration**. Sometimes, the most important information comes through the things they don't say out loud. As you deepen your practice, you'll notice that your own body often mirrors their state: tightness in your chest, a sudden headache, or a wave of emotion. These are invitations—not problems. Learn to sit with them.

Practitioner Tip:

Before the session begins, take a breath and silently ask:

"What is this person's energy asking for today?"

You might receive a feeling, an image, a word, or a sensation in your own body. Trust it.

These awareness tools are not meant to diagnose—they're meant to **connect**. You are not fixing anyone. You are creating a space where they can remember who they are—beyond the grief, beyond the worry, beyond the imbalance.

"The body whispers before it ever speaks. Learn to listen between the words."

Just for today, I will let go of worry and trust the flow of life.

Quick Reference: Elemental Reiki Session Overview

Element	Season	Organs	Chakra Focus	Primary Emotion	Energetic Focus	Key Tools
Water	Winter	Kidneys & Bladder	Root & Sacral	Fear	Grounding, flow, inner trust	Black tourmaline, sandalwood, ocean sounds
Wood	Spring	Liver & Gallbladder	Solar Plexus	Anger	Movement, vision, release	Tiger's eye, rosemary, wind chimes
Fire	Summer	Heart & Small Intestine	Heart	Joy / Mania	Emotional balance, self-expression	Rose quartz, lavender, soft music
Earth	Late Summer	Spleen & Stomach	Solar Plexus & Root	Worry / Overthinking	Digestion, nurturing, grounding	Citrine, ginger, grounding beats
Metal	Autumn	Lungs & Large Intestine	Throat & Third Eye	Grief	Release, breath, clarity	Clear quartz, eucalyptus, silence

Water Element Reiki Layout: Flow, Fear & Rooting Into Trust

Season: Winter / Organs: Kidneys & Bladder / Chakras: Root & Sacral / Emotion: Fear

The Water Element calls us inward—to rest, reflect, and rebuild. This layout supports clients experiencing fear, insecurity, exhaustion, or spiritual depletion. It's ideal during periods of transition, burnout, or when someone feels "frozen" emotionally or energetically.

This session brings **grounding, safety, and deep energetic replenishment**, encouraging the natural flow of life force through the lower chakras and kidneys.

Client Presentation May Include:

- Fatigue, burnout, lack of motivation
- Anxiety, fear of the future, or chronic survival-mode
- Lower back pain, adrenal fatigue, bladder/kidney issues
- Feeling emotionally "numb" or spiritually disconnected

Session Focus:

- Strengthen the Root & Sacral Chakras
- Reconnect to the inner well of trust and stillness
- Release stored fear and restore energetic flow
- Deeply nourish the kidneys and adrenals
- Support emotional safety and nervous system regulation

Suggested Reiki Hand Positions:

1. **Feet** – Grounding & anchoring
2. **Root Chakra (base of spine or pelvis)** – Security & support
3. **Sacral Chakra (below navel)** – Flow, emotional release, and feminine energy
4. **Kidney area (lower back)** – Adrenal restoration, releasing fear
5. **Heart (optional)** – Reconnecting to inner calm and courage
6. **Forehead (Third Eye)** – Trusting inner vision, restoring clarity
7. **Return to feet** – Seal and ground the energy

Just for today, I will let go of worry and trust the flow of life.

Tools to Enhance the Session (Optional):

- **Crystals:** Black tourmaline, smoky quartz, blue kyanite
- **Essential Oils:** Sandalwood, myrrh, vetiver
- **Sound Healing:** Ocean drum, low-frequency tones, silence
- **Visualization Prompt:** Imagine a deep, still lake within the body. Let fear dissolve into its depths.
- **Elemental Affirmations:**
    - *"I am safe."*
    - *"I trust in the flow of life."*
    - *"Stillness restores me."*
    - *"I release fear and root into peace."*
    - *"I am nourished from the inside out."*

"Water teaches us to soften, to surrender, and to find strength in stillness. In this space of quiet trust, the deepest healing begins."

Wood Element Reiki Layout: Growth, Anger & Direction

Season: Spring / Organs: Liver & Gallbladder / Chakra: Solar Plexus / Emotion: Anger

The Wood Element embodies **renewal, movement, and purpose**. This Reiki session is ideal for clients who feel stuck, frustrated, indecisive, or emotionally tense. It helps clear blocked energy, release suppressed anger, and restore the ability to **act with clarity and intention**.

This session supports personal growth by easing internal pressure and reconnecting the client to their **vision, courage, and creative momentum**.

Client Presentation May Include:

- Irritability, frustration, or repressed anger
- Tension in the jaw, shoulders, or sides of the body
- Digestive issues or hormonal imbalances
- Headaches, migraines, or creative blockages
- Difficulty making decisions or moving forward in life

Session Focus:

- Unblock stuck energy and release internal pressure
- Activate Solar Plexus for confidence and clarity
- Calm and regulate Liver/Gallbladder meridians
- Clear emotional stagnation and invite forward motion
- Support assertiveness and healthy boundaries

Just for today, I will let go of worry and trust the flow of life.

Suggested Reiki Hand Positions:

1. **Feet** – Grounding for stable upward growth
2. **Right side of ribcage (Liver area)** – Emotional detox, decision-making
3. **Left shoulder or outer jaw (Gallbladder meridian)** – Releasing tension
4. **Solar Plexus** – Reclaiming power, processing frustration
5. **Forehead (Third Eye)** – Vision, planning, mental clarity
6. **Shoulders or hands** – Releasing burdens, restoring flow
7. **Return to feet** – Grounding into action with peace

Tools to Enhance the Session (Optional):

- **Crystals:** Tiger's eye, bloodstone, malachite
- **Essential Oils:** Rosemary, peppermint, basil
- **Sound Healing:** Wind chimes, flute, or forest sounds
- **Visualization Prompt:** Imagine a young tree growing tall and flexible, rooted but rising freely into the light.
- **Elemental Affirmations:**
    - *"I am strong and flexible."*
    - *"I release what holds me back."*
    - *"My path is clear and open."*
    - *"I am free to grow."*
    - *"I move forward with courage and grace."*

"Like the trees in spring, we are meant to rise, to bend, to reach toward our vision—not by force, but through alignment with the rhythm of life."

Fire Element Reiki Layout: Passion, Joy & Heart Wisdom

Season: Summer / Organs: Heart & Small Intestine / Chakra: Heart / Emotion: Joy / Mania

The Fire Element governs the **heart, spirit, and emotional expression**. This Reiki session is for clients who are emotionally overwhelmed, burned out, anxious, or disconnected from joy. It supports calming hyperactivity, restoring emotional clarity, and reconnecting to the heart's **natural rhythm of joy and rest**.

This session helps regulate Fire energy so that it doesn't burn too hot—or too dim—allowing the client to feel **seen, steady, and soothed**.

Client Presentation May Include:

- Anxiety, insomnia, or emotional highs and lows
- Overexcitement or difficulty slowing down
- Feelings of burnout, emotional numbness, or joylessness
- Heart palpitations, scattered energy, or hypersensitivity
- Overdependence on others for emotional validation

Session Focus:

- Calm and stabilize the Heart Chakra
- Soothe the nervous system and cool emotional overactivity

Just for today, I will let go of worry and trust the flow of life.

- Reconnect to authentic joy and presence
- Regulate the Heart & Small Intestine meridians
- Create space for emotional rest and inner peace

Suggested Reiki Hand Positions:

1. **Hands on the chest (Heart Chakra)** – Emotional healing & spirit connection
2. **Forehead (Third Eye)** – Mental clarity, cooling the mind
3. **Sides of the head or temples** – Calming overthinking and emotional overwhelm
4. **Solar Plexus** – Centering emotional expression and balance
5. **Back of the heart (between the shoulder blades)** – Releasing emotional pressure
6. **Hands and feet** – Grounding and regulating overactive Fire energy
7. **Return to chest or feet** – Reconnect and seal the session

Tools to Enhance the Session (Optional):

- **Crystals:** Rose quartz, lepidolite, garnet
- **Essential Oils:** Lavender, neroli, rose
- **Sound Healing:** Harp, soft bells, birdsong, gentle music in the key of C
- **Visualization Prompt:** Imagine a glowing ember in the heart—not a wildfire, but a steady flame—warming, radiant, and peaceful.
- **Elemental Affirmations:**
  - *"I rest in joy."*
  - *"My heart is open, and I am safe to feel."*

- *"I shine without burning out."*
- *"Joy flows through me with ease."*
- *"My spirit is calm, warm, and whole."*

"Fire teaches us that joy is not a performance. It is a quiet warmth that rises from within when we are aligned with our heart and Spirit."

Earth Element Reiki Layout: Nurturing, Stability & Worry

Season: Late Summer / Organs: Spleen & Stomach / Chakras: Solar Plexus & Root / Emotion: Worry / Overthinking

The Earth Element is the **center of support and self-nourishment**. This Reiki session is ideal for clients who feel mentally scattered, emotionally overextended, or energetically drained from giving too much. It helps anchor the client in their body, calm the mind, and restore a deep sense of **inner peace and trust**.

This layout supports digestion (physical and emotional), eases looping thoughts, and brings the client back to their own **center of gravity**.

Client Presentation May Include:

- Worry, overthinking, or inability to make decisions
- Digestive issues or fatigue after eating
- Feeling ungrounded, spacey, or overly emotional
- Over-caretaking others or lack of boundaries
- Lack of motivation or direction, brain fog

Session Focus:

- Grounding and reconnecting to the body
- Soothing the Solar Plexus and overactive mind
- Supporting the stomach and spleen energetically
- Releasing emotional over-responsibility
- Rebuilding a felt sense of "I am enough"

Suggested Reiki Hand Positions:

1. **Feet or ankles** – Grounding and anchoring scattered energy
2. **Root Chakra (lower abdomen)** – Safety, stability, physical connection
3. **Solar Plexus (upper abdomen)** – Mental clarity, emotional digestion
4. **Stomach area (center of belly)** – Soothing digestive tension and worry
5. **Shoulders or arms** – Releasing burdens and responsibilities
6. **Forehead (optional)** – Quieting looping thoughts and self-doubt
7. **Return to feet or hands** – Closing with steady, nurturing energy

Tools to Enhance the Session (Optional):

- **Crystals:** Citrine, yellow jasper, smoky quartz
- **Essential Oils:** Ginger, sweet orange, chamomile
- **Sound Healing:** Drumming, heartbeat rhythms, earth tones in the key of E
- **Visualization Prompt:** Imagine warm golden light filling the belly and radiating outward, rooting the client into the Earth like a mountain.
- **Elemental Affirmations:**
  - *"I am grounded, supported, and whole."*
  - *"I release worry and return to the present moment."*
  - *"I nourish myself with love and care."*
  - *"My center is steady and strong."*
  - *"I give without losing myself."*

Just for today, I will let go of worry and trust the flow of life.

"Earth reminds us to slow down, to return to the body, and to remember that we are held—by the ground beneath us, and by the nourishment we give ourselves."

Metal Element Reiki Layout: Clarity, Grief & Letting Go

Season: Autumn / Organs: Lungs & Large Intestine / Chakras: Throat & Third Eye / Emotion: Grief

The Metal Element invites us to **release with reverence**—to let go of what no longer serves us so that we can uncover what is precious, true, and enduring. This Reiki session is for clients moving through grief, emotional stagnation, mental clutter, or spiritual disconnection.

It offers sacred space for **breath, clarity, and graceful letting go**. When Metal energy is restored, clients often feel lighter, more focused, and inwardly aligned.

Client Presentation May Include:

- Unresolved grief or sadness
- Difficulty letting go of people, emotions, or expectations
- Shallow breathing, chest tightness, or throat constriction
- A sense of dullness, disconnection, or spiritual fatigue
- Cluttered thoughts or perfectionism

Session Focus:

- Clear and open the lungs and throat
- Support emotional release and expression
- Restore breath and clarity
- Release grief or attachments stored in the body

Just for today, I will let go of worry and trust the flow of life.

- Reconnect to inner value and spiritual perspective

Suggested Reiki Hand Positions:

1. **Hands on the chest (Lung area)** – Breath, presence, emotional clarity
2. **Throat Chakra** – Expression of grief, release of suppressed emotion
3. **Sides of the neck or jaw** – Softening tension and emotional holding
4. **Third Eye** – Insight, spiritual clarity, new vision
5. **Abdomen (Large Intestine region)** – Releasing waste, emotional purging
6. **Shoulders or back of the heart** – Grief support and energetic lightening
7. **Return to feet or hands** – Grounding clarity and sealing the session

Tools to Enhance the Session (Optional):

- **Crystals:** Clear quartz, selenite, herkimer diamond
- **Essential Oils:** Eucalyptus, frankincense, white sage
- **Sound Healing:** Silence, wind sounds, soft metal bowls in the key of G
- **Visualization Prompt:** Imagine golden autumn leaves gently falling from a tree—each one a letting go. The tree remains rooted, clear, and open to light.
- **Elemental Affirmations:**
  - *"I release with love and grace."*
  - *"Each breath brings clarity and peace."*
  - *"Grief is not weakness—it is love moving through me."*
  - *"I make space for what truly matters."*

o   *"In stillness, I remember my worth."*

"Metal teaches us that letting go is not an ending—it's a sacred refinement. It clears the way for truth, light, and inner peace to rise once again."

Just for today, I will let go of worry and trust the flow of life.

Blending Each Element with Sound Healing, Aromatherapy & Crystals

Amplifying the Frequency of Healing Through Elemental Tools

While Reiki in its purest form requires only your intention and connection, incorporating supportive tools like **sound healing, aromatherapy, and crystals** can enhance the elemental resonance of your session. These vibrational allies speak the language of energy—each with their own unique frequency that can **amplify, balance, or soothe** the elements within the body and auric field.

When used intuitively, these tools help attune the client to the **natural rhythms of Earth, Air, Fire, Water, and Wood**— making the session more sensory-rich, personalized, and energetically aligned.

Water Element – Stillness, Depth & Flow

- **Sound Healing:** Ocean drum, deep crystal bowls (note D), rainsticks, or recordings of gentle waves
- **Aromatherapy:** Sandalwood, myrrh, vetiver, clary sage (deeply grounding & reflective)
- **Crystals:** Black tourmaline (protection), moonstone (emotional balance), aquamarine (flow)
- **Use For:** Releasing fear, restoring trust, encouraging emotional flow, nervous system regulation

Wood Element – Growth, Vision & Movement

- **Sound Healing:** Bamboo chimes, flute, wind sounds, or tuning forks in note E
- **Aromatherapy:** Rosemary (mental clarity), peppermint (movement), basil (focus)
- **Crystals:** Bloodstone (action), malachite (release), green aventurine (renewal)
- **Use For:** Creative blocks, emotional stagnation, frustration, liver cleansing, decision-making

Fire Element – Passion, Joy & Heart Expression

- **Sound Healing:** Harp, singing bowls in note C or F, birdsong, soft bells
- **Aromatherapy:** Lavender (cooling), neroli (heart-opening), rose (emotional healing)
- **Crystals:** Rose quartz (unconditional love), garnet (vitality), lepidolite (emotional balance)
- **Use For:** Anxiety, emotional highs/lows, burnout, reconnecting to joy or heart purpose

Earth Element – Grounding, Nourishment & Centering

- **Sound Healing:** Steady drumming, heartbeat rhythms, bowls in note G or E
- **Aromatherapy:** Ginger (digestion), sweet orange (uplift), cardamom (comfort), patchouli (grounding)
- **Crystals:** Citrine (confidence), yellow jasper (stability), smoky quartz (grounding)
- **Use For:** Overthinking, worry, mental fatigue, feeling unsupported or ungrounded

Just for today, I will let go of worry and trust the flow of life.

Metal Element – Clarity, Grief & Letting Go

- **Sound Healing:** Tingsha bells, wind chimes, metal bowls in note A, silence
- **Aromatherapy:** Eucalyptus (lungs), frankincense (spiritual clarity), white sage (clearing)
- **Crystals:** Clear quartz (amplification), selenite (purification), herkimer diamond (lightness)
- **Use For:** Grief, emotional release, spiritual clarity, decluttering mind and body

How to Integrate These Tools in Session:

- Use sound or oils **at the beginning** of a session to set the tone and invite the element's energy in.
- Place a crystal **on or near a chakra** that corresponds with the element being worked on.
- Diffuse oils, place a drop on the client's palms or feet (with permission), or blend into a post-session **elemental mist**.
- Play soft sound healing tracks (live or recorded) in the **key of the related chakra/element**.
- Encourage the client to **visualize the element** through sound, scent, and touch as you hold Reiki positions.

"Each tool is a doorway. Through sound, scent, and stone, the elements awaken. Reiki flows where nature remembers itself."

Elemental Tool Reference Chart

Sound, Scent & Stone for Reiki Healing

Element	Sound Healing	Aromatherapy	Crystals	Primary Chakra(s)	Supports
Water	Ocean drum, rainstick, bowls (note D)	Sandalwood, vetiver, myrrh, clary sage	Black tourmaline, moonstone, aquamarine	Root & Sacral	Fear, trust, deep rest, emotional flow
Wood	Bamboo chimes, flute, tuning forks (E)	Rosemary, peppermint, basil	Bloodstone, malachite, green aventurine	Solar Plexus	Frustration, stagnation, growth, vision
Fire	Harp, bells, birdsong, bowls (C or F)	Lavender, rose, neroli	Rose quartz, garnet, lepidolite	Heart	Joy, burnout, emotional balance, connection
Earth	Drumming, heartbeat rhythms, bowls (G or E)	Ginger, sweet orange, cardamom, patchouli	Citrine, yellow jasper, smoky quartz	Root & Solar Plexus	Overthinking, worry, nourishment, grounding
Metal	Tingsha, wind chimes, metal bowls (A)	Eucalyptus, frankincense, white sage	Clear quartz, selenite, herkimer diamond	Throat & Third Eye	Grief, letting go, breath, clarity

Just for today, I will let go of worry and trust the flow of life.

Chapter 10: The Seasons Within – A Year of Elemental Reiki

Elemental Reiki Flow: A Signature Session Journey

A Step-by-Step Framework Integrating Reiki with the Five Elements

This Elemental Reiki session is more than a healing—it's a **guided energetic story**, designed to bring the client into harmony with themselves and the natural world. Each element represents a **phase of transformation**, and together, they form a complete energetic circuit.

You can follow this framework in full, or intuitively pause and deepen where your client's energy calls for attention.

1. Begin with Elemental Assessment

Create awareness and choose the element(s) that need support.

Before starting the session:

- Ask a few key questions (or use the intake form).
- Use muscle testing, breath observation, or facial cues.
- Let your intuition guide you—what *feels* out of balance?
- Optional: Pull an Elemental Oracle Card or chakra card to guide focus.

This step helps the client feel seen, and gives you an energetic compass for the session.

2. Grounding the Body – Earth Element

Focus: Stability, support, digestion, overthinking

Begin the session by calling in the Earth element to create grounding, safety, and presence.

Reiki Hand Positions:

- Feet, knees, or base of spine
- Solar Plexus and Root Chakra
- Optional: Place a smoky quartz or citrine crystal on the abdomen

Use affirmations:

"I am grounded."
"I am supported by the Earth."

This sets a stable foundation and clears mental clutter or energetic overload.

Just for today, I will let go of worry and trust the flow of life.

3. Clearing Flow – Water Element

Focus: Emotional release, fear, subconscious blocks

Next, move into the **Water Element**, helping energy begin to flow and release.

Reiki Hand Positions:

- Sacral Chakra, lower back, and kidneys
- Optional: Add deep breathing or visualizations of a flowing river

Use affirmations:

"I trust the flow of life."
"I release what I no longer need."

Water helps soften, soothe, and begin emotional integration.

4. Reclaiming Direction – Wood Element

Focus: Growth, decision-making, life path

This phase supports clients who feel stuck or uncertain. Wood energy restores movement and direction.

Reiki Hand Positions:

- Liver/gallbladder region, Solar Plexus, or shoulders
- Visualize green light expanding upward like a tree
- Gently stretch or invite movement into the body if appropriate

Use affirmations:

"I grow with purpose."
"I am ready to move forward."

Wood awakens inner vision, creative energy, and courage.

5. Igniting Joy – Fire Element

Focus: Joy, heart healing, expression

Here you activate the emotional heart and soul's radiance.

Reiki Hand Positions:

- Heart chakra, hands, or forehead
- Visualize golden or pink light radiating from the chest outward
- Encourage breath and expansion

Use affirmations:

"I shine from within."
"My heart is open and joyful."

Fire invites connection, compassion, and vitality.

6. Releasing & Refining – Metal Element

Focus: Grief, clarity, breath, spiritual connection

This is the final phase before sealing—an opportunity to release old patterns and integrate clarity.

Just for today, I will let go of worry and trust the flow of life.

Reiki Hand Positions:

- Throat and Third Eye
- Gentle breathwork or silent pauses
- Optional: Use frankincense oil or selenite for lightness

Use affirmations:

"I let go with grace."
"I breathe in clarity."

Metal clears out lingering heaviness and sharpens spiritual awareness.

7. Seal the Session – Integration & Blessing

Close with intentional energy and grounding

- Sweep the aura from head to feet to smooth the field.
- Seal the session with an **elemental affirmation** based on the dominant energy.
- Place one hand on the heart and one on the Root Chakra.
- Gently ground the client by touching their feet or placing stones near them.

Final Words (spoken silently or aloud):

"Balance is restored. The elements are in harmony. You are whole."

Optional: Offer a journaling prompt or elemental card as a takeaway.

Why This Framework Works

Structured yet intuitive: Offers flow and order, but allows for flexibility based on what arises.
Naturally complete: Follows a full energetic cycle, from grounding to release to spiritual clarity.
Client-centered: Emotionally resonant and visually symbolic—helps clients understand their own energy.
Signature method: Gives your Reiki practice a unique, nature-aligned identity that clients will remember.

Just for today, I will let go of worry and trust the flow of life.

Introduction to the Elemental Energy Map

Seeing the Body as a Living Elemental Landscape

The body is more than muscle and bone—it is a living, breathing ecosystem made of elemental forces. Just as the Earth is shaped by water, fire, wind, wood, and stone, so too is the human energy system.

In Reiki, we work with the unseen flow of life force. In the Five Element tradition, we understand that this flow takes on distinct qualities: **the rooted strength of Earth, the flowing adaptability of Water, the expanding drive of Wood, the expressive warmth of Fire, and the refining breath of Metal.** These elements are not just poetic metaphors—they are active energies that express through our organs, emotions, joints, and chakras.

The **Elemental Energy Map** brings this wisdom to life by showing you where each element lives in the body—and how to read its signs of harmony or imbalance. This visual guide is more than just a chart. It is an energetic mirror that reveals where your client is thriving, where they are stuck, and how to restore flow using intuitive, element-based Reiki.

Whether you're a seasoned practitioner or just beginning to blend Reiki with the Five Elements, this map offers a new way to *see and serve* the body—with nature as your blueprint.

WATER ELEMENT

Winter	Flow, restoration, deep emotional memory
Main emotion	Fear
Chakra	Root & Sacral
Organ	Kidneys & Bladder

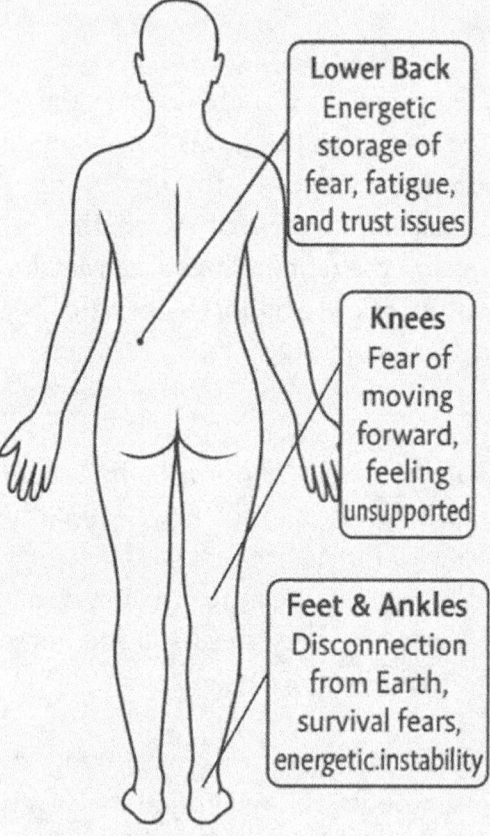

Lower Back
Energetic storage of fear, fatigue, and trust issues

Knees
Fear of moving forward, feeling unsupported

Feet & Ankles
Disconnection from Earth, survival fears, energetic.instability

◆ **Crystals:**
Black tourmaline, moonstone

◐ **Essential oils:**
Cedarwood, sandalwood

♥ **Affirmations:**
- I trust the flow of life.
- I am safe, grounded, and supported.
- I restore my energy in stillness.

Use Water Element focus when your client is experiencing:
- Exhaustion or burnout
- Chronic lower back pain
- Feeling disconnected, or anxious
- Difficulty resting, anscious

Just for today, I will let go of worry and trust the flow of life.

Water Element

- **Chakras:** Root & Sacral
- **Joints/Regions:** Hips, lower back, knees, bladder
- **Organs:** Kidneys & Bladder
- **Emotion:** Fear, insecurity, exhaustion
- **Imbalances may show as:**
  - Adrenal fatigue, back pain, urinary issues, emotional shutdown
  - Difficulty resting, trusting, or flowing with change
- **Balancing Reiki Positions:**
  - Lower back, sacral area, feet
  - Use visualizations of flowing water
  - Support with water element affirmations & breathing

WOOD ELEMENT

Element: Wood

Season: Spring

Primary Energy
Growth, Direction, Expansion

Main Emotion: Anger

Chakra: Solar Plexus Chakra

Meridians:
Liver & Gallbladder

Personality Traits
Driven, determined, confident, ambitious

Governs: Direction, movement, motivation, vision

Frustration, irritability, headaches

Stored tension and anger, rigidity and impatience

Resistance to change, feeling stuck

Lack of direction, imbalance, inaction

Elemental Markers
● Color: Green

Crystals: Amethyst, Green Aventurine, Malachite

Essential oils: Pine, Juniper, Rosemary

I embrace change with flexibility.

I release anger, I choose growth I move forward with purpose

Just for today, I will let go of worry and trust the flow of life.

Wood Element

- **Chakras:** Solar Plexus
- **Joints/Regions:** Liver area, shoulders, neck, jaw
- **Organs:** Liver & Gallbladder
- **Emotion:** Anger, frustration, indecision
- **Imbalances may show as:**
    - Tension in neck or jaw, headaches, digestive bile issues
    - Feeling stuck or directionless
- **Balancing Reiki Positions:**
    - Hands on Solar Plexus, shoulders, or temples
    - Encourage upward, rooted energy like a growing tree
    - Use green crystals or oils like rosemary & basil

🔥 FIRE ELEMENT

SUMMER
PRIMARY ENERGY: JOY,
PASSION, LOVE
MAIN EMOTION: JOY
CHAKRA: HEART

ORGANS: HEART &
SMALL INTESTINE (YANG)
MERIDIANS: HEART (YIN),
SMALL INTESTINE (YANG)
PERSONALITY TRAITS:
CHARISMATIC, DRIVEN, EXPRESSIVE
GOVERNS: COMMUNICA-
TION, CONNECTION

HEAD

Overthinking, burnout,
feelings of overwhelm

CHEST
(HEART CHAKRA)

Heartache, emotional
wounds, lack of joy

ELEMENTAL
MARKERS

● Color

▮ Carnelian,
sunstone

● Ginger

ABDOMEN
(SMALL INTESTINE)

Digestive issues,
blocked enthusiasm,
impatience

AFFIMAIONS

- I ignite my inner light.
- I love fully and joyfully.
- I burn away what does
  not serve me

QUICK USE GUIDE

USE FIRE ELEMENT
focus when your
client is experiencing:

Joylessness,
lack of motivation

High stress, overw-
helm, burnout

Just for today, I will let go of worry and trust the flow of life.

Fire Element

- **Chakras:** Heart & Third Eye
- **Joints/Regions:** Heart center, chest, hands, eyes
- **Organs:** Heart & Small Intestine
- **Emotion:** Joy, mania, emotional overload
- **Imbalances may show as:**
  - Anxiety, heart palpitations, insomnia, social burnout
  - Over-giving or loss of joy
- **Balancing Reiki Positions:**
  - Heart center, palms, forehead
  - Use rose quartz, gold light visualizations, citrus or floral oils
  - Breathwork with focus on softening the chest

EARTH ELEMENT

Late Summer
Main Emotion: Worry
Chakras: Solar Plexus & Root
Organs: Spleen & Stomach
Meridians: Stomach (Yang) & Spleen (Yin)

Indecision,
rumination,
low self-esteem

Digestive issues,
emotional eating

Anxiety about
finances, lack
of stability

Unrooted,
insecure,
overthinking

Aiffirmations:
I am stable
and supported

I am stable and
supported

Quick Use Guide

I am stable and supported
I nourish myself with care
My mind and body are grounded

Use Earth Element focus
for grounding, stabilizing, or
calming an overactive mind

Just for today, I will let go of worry and trust the flow of life.

Earth Element

- **Chakras:** Root & Solar Plexus
- **Joints/Regions:** Knees, feet, stomach, thighs
- **Organs:** Spleen & Stomach
- **Emotion:** Worry, overthinking, need for control
- **Imbalances may show as:**
  - Digestive issues, heaviness, lack of motivation, anxiety
  - Difficulty feeling grounded or supported
- **Balancing Reiki Positions:**
  - Hands on abdomen, feet, or lower legs
  - Root-to-Solar Plexus sweep
  - Use earth tones, grounding crystals, vetiver or patchouli oils

METAL ELEMENT

Season — **Autumn**

Main emotion — **Grief**

Chakras — **Throat & Third Eye**

Organ — **Lungs & Large Intestine**

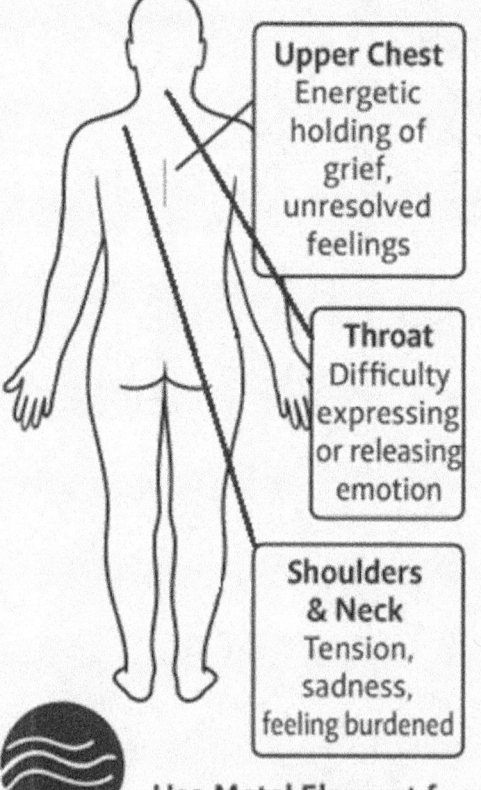

Upper Chest
Energetic holding of grief, unresolved feelings

Throat
Difficulty expressing or releasing emotion

Shoulders & Neck
Tension, sadness, feeling burdened

◆ **Crystals:**
Selenite
Clear quartz

◆ **Essential oils:**
Eucalyptus,
Peppermint
Frankincense

♥ **Affirmations:**
- I release what no longer serves me
- I find clarity through breath and stillness
- I forgive and find peace in my heart

Use Metal Element focus when your client is experiencing:

- Unprocessed grief or sadness · Isolation or disconnection
- Difficulty letting go · Burdened by unresolved emotions

Just for today, I will let go of worry and trust the flow of life.

Metal Element

- **Chakras:** Throat & Third Eye
- **Joints/Regions:** Lungs, upper chest, throat, jaw
- **Organs:** Lungs & Large Intestine
- **Emotion:** Grief, resistance, lack of clarity
- **Imbalances may show as:**
  o Shortness of breath, skin issues, constipation
  o Difficulty letting go (physically or emotionally)
- **Balancing Reiki Positions:**
  o Throat, Third Eye, upper chest
  o Visualize mist, breath, or silver light
  o Use frankincense, eucalyptus, or selenite

How to Use the Elemental Energy Map in Practice

The **Elemental Energy Map** is designed to help you connect physical symptoms, emotional patterns, and energetic imbalances to the wisdom of the Five Elements. Whether you're a Reiki practitioner, student, or someone on a personal healing journey, the map offers a clear and intuitive way to bring insight into your sessions.

For Reiki Practitioners

Use the Elemental Map to bring depth, precision, and nature-based wisdom into your healing work.

Step-by-Step:

1. **Begin with Client Intake:**
    Use the map to guide your intake conversation. Ask about areas of physical discomfort, emotional patterns, or stress. Mark these on the body grid.
2. **Observe and Cross-Reference:**
    Match symptoms to their elemental zones (e.g., shoulder tension = Wood element). Use the map to see the underlying emotional or energetic story.
3. **Design the Session Flow:**
    Use the map to determine where to start, where to focus, and how to move through the session. Follow the elemental cycle (Water → Wood → Fire → Earth → Metal) if needed.
4. **Choose Reiki Hand Placements Intuitively:**
    The map offers chakra, joint, and organ associations

Just for today, I will let go of worry and trust the flow of life.

for each element. Use it to inform your hand placements, visualizations, affirmations, or tool use (e.g., crystals, oils).

5. **Empower the Client:**
   After the session, show them the map (if appropriate). Explain what you found and how the elements relate to their experience. Invite them into the process of understanding their body as an energetic landscape.

For Clients, Students & Self-Practitioners

The map isn't just for practitioners—it's a powerful self-awareness tool.

Step-by-Step:

1. **Body Check-In:**
   Take a quiet moment to scan your body. Where do you feel discomfort, tension, or emotion? Place a finger or symbol on the map to represent it.

2. **Identify Elemental Themes:**
   Using the legend or reference guide, locate which elements govern those areas. Reflect on the related emotions, seasons, and patterns.

3. **Journal or Reflect:**
   Ask yourself:
   - What might this element be trying to teach me?
   - Where do I need more balance, flow, or release?
   - Which archetype (Dreamer, Visionary, etc.) resonates with what I'm feeling?

4. **Choose a Healing Focus:**
   Use the map to guide a self-Reiki session, meditation, breathwork, or intention-setting based on what your body and energy are showing you.
5. **Track Your Shifts:**
   Use a blank map to mark how your energy changes over time—physically, emotionally, spiritually. Watch your healing journey unfold.

Just for today, I will let go of worry and trust the flow of life.

Elemental Reiki Archetypes

The Energetic Soul of the Five Elements

Each of the Five Elements—Water, Wood, Fire, Earth, and Metal—carries more than just physical or emotional associations. They also represent distinct **archetypal energies**—soul-level guides that live within each of us.

These archetypes are not characters we "become," but rather **facets of our higher self** we can access, embody, and learn from in times of imbalance, healing, or spiritual growth. They reflect how each element expresses itself through our thoughts, emotions, choices, and healing paths.

- The **Water archetype** listens deeply and dreams inward.
- The **Wood archetype** seeks direction and pushes toward growth.
- The **Fire archetype** radiates joy and emotional expression.
- The **Earth archetype** nurtures, grounds, and stabilizes.
- The **Metal archetype** lets go with grace and connects to the sacred.

As you work with Reiki and the Five Elements, these archetypes can serve as **energetic guides** for both you and your clients. They bring personality and depth to the practice—offering insight into where healing is needed, how to approach it with compassion, and which inner strength is ready to rise.

These archetypes can be used in a variety of ways:

- As a **lens for self-reflection** or journaling
- As a **guide for setting session intentions**
- As a way to **understand your client's elemental needs or emotional patterns**
- As a tool for deepening your connection to the elements in daily life

You may notice that you're drawn to one archetype more than others—or that you shift between them depending on the season, your energy state, or what's unfolding in your life. This is not only natural—it's exactly how the elemental cycle is meant to flow.

As you explore the following archetypes, consider:

Which part of you is asking to be seen?
Which energy wants to speak through your hands, your heart, or your voice?
Which inner guide is ready to return you to balance?

Let these archetypes be your teachers.
Let Reiki be the bridge.
And let nature speak through your healing hands.

Just for today, I will let go of worry and trust the flow of life.

Water Archetype:
The Dreamer / Deep Listener

"Still waters run deep."

The **Water Element** is the soul of stillness, reflection, and inner truth. As an archetype, the Dreamer or Deep Listener represents the part of us that surrenders to the unknown, communes with intuition, and trusts the unseen. This guide teaches us the art of resting, dreaming, and listening—not just with our ears, but with our spirit.

When this Archetype is in Balance:

- You are deeply intuitive and emotionally attuned.
- You trust your inner voice and make time for solitude.
- You're able to hold sacred space for others with calm and quiet wisdom.
- Your dreams, meditations, and energy sessions flow effortlessly.
- You replenish your energy through rest, stillness, or spiritual practices.

When this Archetype is Out of Balance:

- You may feel emotionally overwhelmed or shut down.
- Fear blocks forward movement.
- You withdraw, isolate, or feel drained and disconnected.

- You experience burnout from giving too much without restoring.
- You ignore intuitive messages in favor of "logic" or fear-based control.

The Reiki Wisdom of the Dreamer:

The Dreamer archetype reminds us that healing is not always active—it is often receptive. In Reiki practice, this archetype helps the practitioner **become the vessel** for healing, rather than the doer. It teaches the power of quiet presence, deep listening, and flowing *with* the energy, rather than trying to direct it.

During Reiki sessions aligned with Water, you may:

- Focus on **calming the nervous system**
- Help clients **release long-held emotional tension**
- Use **dreamwork, breathwork, or meditation** to deepen awareness
- Place hands gently on the **lower back, kidneys, and sacral chakra**
- Encourage silence, soft music, or water sounds during treatment

Affirmations of the Water Archetype:

"I listen to the wisdom beneath the surface."
"I allow the flow to guide me."
"Stillness is my strength."
"I trust what I feel, even if I cannot see it."

Just for today, I will let go of worry and trust the flow of life.

The **Dreamer / Deep Listener** archetype is a perfect energetic guide for clients or practitioners going through emotional healing, burnout recovery, or spiritual uncertainty. It encourages slowing down, honoring your energy cycles, and embracing the mystery of the unknown.

Are You Embodying the Water Archetype?

The Dreamer / Deep Listener

Answer the following questions with **Yes**, **Sometimes**, or **No**. Tally your answers at the end to reveal your current elemental influence.

Emotional Flow & Intuition

1. Do you crave solitude, rest, or retreat more than usual?
2. Do you find yourself emotionally sensitive, even without a clear reason?
3. Do you experience vivid dreams or intuitive "hits" you can't explain?
4. Are you more introverted or drawn to internal processing right now?
5. Do you feel emotions deeply but struggle to express them outwardly?

Physical & Energetic Clues

6. Are you experiencing lower back pain, fatigue, or tension in your kidneys or hips?
7. Have you noticed disrupted sleep or feeling unrefreshed upon waking?

8. Do you feel energetically "drained," as if you've been pouring from an empty cup?
9. Are you avoiding movement, action, or decision-making out of fear or overwhelm?
10. Are you easily startled or carrying a sense of underlying fear or nervous tension?

Spiritual Themes

11. Are you currently navigating a period of uncertainty or spiritual transformation?
12. Do you feel called to slow down, meditate, or reconnect with your inner voice?
13. Are you exploring your emotional past or trying to release long-held fear?
14. Do you feel deeply connected to the energy of water, the moon, or winter?
15. Do you often act as the emotional anchor or "space holder" for others?

Scoring

- **Mostly YES:** You are currently **embodying the Water Archetype**. It may be time to rest, restore, and reconnect with your intuition. Focus on stillness, gentle movement, emotional release, and trusting your inner voice.
- **Mostly SOMETIMES:** The Water energy is **active but not dominant**. You may be in transition, needing brief moments of stillness or deeper emotional reflection. Listening inward will reveal what's needed.
- **Mostly NO:** Water may be **underactive or calling for attention**. You might be moving too fast, avoiding

Just for today, I will let go of worry and trust the flow of life.

emotions, or disconnected from rest and restoration. Consider introducing Water element practices to rebalance.

Your Water Practices

If this archetype is strong for you, try:

- Gentle Reiki over the kidneys, sacral, and feet
- Moon rituals, salt baths, or dream journaling
- Drinking more water with intention
- Meditation on stillness or trust
- Affirmation: *"I flow with ease. I trust the unknown."*

Wood Archetype: The Visionary / Pathfinder

"I know where I'm going—and I grow toward it."

The **Wood Element** governs vision, movement, and direction. As an archetype, the **Visionary** or **Pathfinder** represents your ability to see beyond obstacles and take purposeful action. It is the spark of **creative clarity**, the courage to grow, and the strength to break through what once held you back.

When this Archetype is in Balance:

- You feel inspired, purposeful, and driven by a clear inner mission.
- You're able to make decisions with confidence and follow through.
- You see challenges as opportunities for growth.
- Your energy rises in healthy, focused momentum.
- You take aligned action without aggression or burnout.

When this Archetype is Out of Balance:

- You may feel stuck, directionless, or overwhelmed with options.
- Anger or irritability surfaces easily when your path feels blocked.
- You resist change or fear making the wrong move.
- You push too hard or become impatient with the process.

Just for today, I will let go of worry and trust the flow of life.

- Digestive issues or headaches may arise from inner tension.

The Reiki Wisdom of the Visionary:

The Pathfinder archetype brings **momentum** to the Reiki session. It helps release energetic stagnation and encourages movement—whether physical, emotional, or spiritual. This is the archetype of **breakthrough energy**, especially for clients who feel blocked, frustrated, or unable to access their purpose.

In Reiki sessions focused on Wood energy:

- Place hands on the **Solar Plexus, shoulders**, or **liver area**
- Encourage upward, rooted visualization—like a tree growing toward the light
- Use breathwork to release emotional tension and reclaim personal power
- Incorporate green crystals (like aventurine) or essential oils (like rosemary or basil)

Affirmations of the Wood Archetype:

"I grow through challenge."
"I trust my path and take action with clarity."
"I release what holds me back."
"My energy flows freely toward my vision."

The **Visionary / Pathfinder** archetype is especially helpful when working with clients navigating major life changes, facing indecision, or healing from suppressed anger. It helps them reorient their energy and remember: **they are not stuck—they are growing.**

Are You Embodying the Wood Archetype?

The Visionary / Pathfinder

Answer each question with **Yes**, **Sometimes**, or **No**. This quiz helps reveal whether the energy of **Wood** is currently dominant, imbalanced, or in need of support.

Mental & Emotional Flow

1. Do you feel a strong urge to move forward, make a change, or start something new?
2. Are you full of ideas but struggling to focus or follow through?
3. Do you get easily irritated when things don't go as planned?
4. Do you often feel "stuck" or frustrated in a situation you can't control?
5. Do you find decision-making to be a source of tension or stress?

Physical & Energetic Clues

6. Are you experiencing tightness in your shoulders, neck, or jaw?
7. Do you have digestive issues, particularly related to the liver or gallbladder?

Just for today, I will let go of worry and trust the flow of life.

8. Do you wake up feeling restless, like something in you is ready to shift?
9. Are you clenching your teeth or feeling internal pressure to "get things done"?
10. Do you notice a surge of energy in springtime or a sense of renewal during seasonal shifts?

Spiritual & Life Direction Themes

11. Are you seeking clarity about your life's direction or purpose?
12. Do you feel ready to grow but unsure of where to begin?
13. Do you feel blocked creatively or disconnected from your vision?
14. Are you noticing patterns of procrastination or bursts of anger?
15. Do you resonate with the image of a tree: rooted, yet always reaching?

Scoring

- **Mostly YES:** You are strongly embodying the **Wood Archetype**. It's time to channel that energy into creative visioning, focused growth, and clearing internal resistance. Ground your ideas in action and allow space for flexibility.
- **Mostly SOMETIMES:** Wood energy is present, but not fully integrated. You may be on the cusp of a breakthrough—pause, plan, and take aligned steps.
- **Mostly NO:** Wood may be underactive or out of balance. You might be stuck, disconnected from your

vision, or suppressing anger. Invite movement, flexibility, and purpose back into your energetic field.

Your Wood Practices

If this archetype resonates with you, try:

- Reiki over the Solar Plexus, shoulders, or liver area
- Journaling to clarify goals and release frustration
- Walking in nature or engaging in light movement/stretching
- Liver-cleansing foods and lemon water
- Affirmation: *"I grow with purpose. I move forward with clarity."*

Just for today, I will let go of worry and trust the flow of life.

Fire Archetype: The Lover / Joyful Creator

"I radiate warmth, connection, and creative passion."

The **Fire Element** governs the heart, joy, expression, and spiritual connection. As an archetype, the **Lover** or **Joyful Creator** represents your capacity to love deeply, express authentically, and shine your inner light. This is the energy of emotional presence, **soul-level enthusiasm**, and relational harmony.

When this Archetype is in Balance:

- You feel joyful, playful, and alive.
- Your heart is open—ready to give and receive love freely.
- You are comfortable being seen, expressing your truth, and connecting with others.
- Your emotions feel vibrant but steady.
- You're in touch with your creative spark and spiritual purpose.

When this Archetype is Out of Balance:

- You may feel emotionally exhausted, anxious, or disconnected.
- You might overextend yourself, give too much, or seek validation through others.
- Emotional expression feels overwhelming, chaotic, or suppressed.

- You could experience insomnia, heart palpitations, or heat in the body.
- Joy feels out of reach—even when everything looks "fine" on the outside.

The Reiki Wisdom of the Joyful Creator:

In Reiki, the Lover archetype brings healing to the **emotional heart**, rekindling warmth where numbness, grief, or burnout may have taken hold. It also invites the practitioner to **be fully present**—not just channeling energy, but holding space with compassion, curiosity, and joy.

Reiki sessions working with Fire energy may include:

- Hands on the **Heart Chakra, palms,** or **forehead (Third Eye)**
- Visualizing golden light radiating from the heart outward
- Using rose quartz, pink tourmaline, or heart-based essential oils like rose or neroli
- Soft, uplifting music or silence to allow the heart to speak

Affirmations of the Fire Archetype:

"I am a radiant light of love and joy."
"It is safe to feel, express, and connect."
"My heart is open and protected."
"I create with love, and I shine with purpose."

Just for today, I will let go of worry and trust the flow of life.

REIKI AND THE FIVE ELEMENTS 171

The **Lover / Joyful Creator** archetype is powerful for sessions involving heartbreak, social anxiety, burnout, or lack of inspiration. It helps clients return to their **emotional center**, embrace their gifts, and radiate warmth from the inside out.

Are You Embodying the Fire Archetype?

The Lover / Joyful Creator

Answer the following with **Yes, Sometimes**, or **No**.
This quiz will help you discover if the **Fire Element**—the energy of passion, joy, and heart-centered expression—is dominant, in balance, or in need of attention.

Emotional & Relational Energy

1. Do you feel emotionally open, expressive, or inspired to connect with others?
2. Are you seeking more joy, fun, or creative expression in your life?
3. Do you tend to give a lot of emotional energy to others—even when you feel drained?
4. Do you often feel emotionally overstimulated, overwhelmed, or "burned out"?
5. Are your relationships currently a source of deep passion or emotional confusion?

Physical & Energetic Clues

6. Are you experiencing restlessness, insomnia, or difficulty "cooling down" emotionally or mentally?
7. Do you notice tension or heat in your chest, hands, or eyes?

8. Are you speaking rapidly or emotionally, even when you don't intend to?
9. Do you experience heart palpitations, shallow breathing, or surges of excitement or anxiety?
10. Do you feel unusually "lit up"—or burnt out?

Spiritual & Creative Themes

11. Are you craving a deeper connection to your purpose, passion, or inner fire?
12. Do you feel a strong desire to create, perform, or share your gifts with the world?
13. Are you feeling emotionally raw, heartbroken, or disconnected from joy?
14. Do you struggle to hold emotional boundaries or "take on" others' energy?
15. Do you feel drawn to fire, sunlight, dancing, or being seen?

Scoring

- **Mostly YES:** You are currently embodying the **Fire Archetype**. Embrace this time for creative expression, joy, emotional release, and heart healing. Just be mindful to protect your energy and avoid overgiving.
- **Mostly SOMETIMES:** Fire is active but fluctuating. Nurture your inner flame without overextending. Rest, play, and reconnect to what lights you up.
- **Mostly NO:** Fire may be depleted or blocked. You could be emotionally closed off, burned out, or holding back your passion. It's time to rekindle your joy and remember what makes your heart come alive.

Just for today, I will let go of worry and trust the flow of life.

Your Fire Practices

To restore or balance this archetype:

- Reiki hand positions over the **Heart Chakra, hands,** and **forehead**
- Dance, create art, or spend time in warm, joyful spaces
- Use heart-opening essential oils like rose or neroli
- Wear or meditate with red, pink, or gold tones
- Affirmation: *"I shine with joy. My heart is open and safe."*

Earth Archetype: The Caregiver / Stabilizer

"I am rooted, whole, and enough."

The **Earth Element** governs nourishment, stability, support, and inner peace. As an archetype, the **Caregiver** or **Stabilizer** reflects your ability to hold space, offer compassion, and feel grounded in your body and life. This is the steady energy of nurturance—**being held and holding others** in safe, balanced care.

When this Archetype is in Balance:

- You feel grounded, centered, and emotionally stable.
- You can give to others without draining yourself.
- Your digestion—both physical and emotional—is strong and resilient.
- You feel connected to your body, your home, and the present moment.
- You offer comfort, structure, and care with loving boundaries.

When this Archetype is Out of Balance:

- You may feel overwhelmed by responsibility or emotionally heavy.
- Worry, rumination, or overthinking dominate your mental space.
- You tend to over-give, neglect your own needs, or feel drained by caretaking.

Just for today, I will let go of worry and trust the flow of life.

- You may experience digestive issues, fatigue, or physical heaviness.
- Disconnection from the body or over-attachment to routines may occur.

The Reiki Wisdom of the Caregiver:

This archetype invites the practitioner to become a **safe container**—one who grounds chaotic energy, holds emotional space, and restores energetic nourishment. In Elemental Reiki, this energy is especially helpful for those who are ungrounded, overburdened, or caught in cycles of stress and overthinking.

During Earth-focused Reiki sessions:

- Place hands on the **Solar Plexus**, **abdomen**, **knees**, or **feet**
- Use grounding visualizations—imagine roots growing from the body into the earth
- Support with stones like hematite, citrine, or jasper
- Use essential oils such as ginger, patchouli, or vetiver

Affirmations of the Earth Archetype:

"I am safe, supported, and at peace."
"I nourish myself as I care for others."
"Worry dissolves as I return to stillness."
"I trust the rhythm of my body and life."

The **Caregiver / Stabilizer** archetype is especially useful when working with clients who are emotionally fatigued, mentally scattered, or physically imbalanced. It teaches the power of slowing down, **returning to center**, and remembering: healing often begins with being held.

Are You Embodying the Earth Archetype?

The Caregiver / Stabilizer

Use **Yes, Sometimes,** or **No** to respond to the questions below.
This quiz helps you explore whether the **Earth Element**—the energy of support, grounding, and nourishment—is currently active, balanced, or in need of attention.

Emotional & Mental Themes

1. Do you often find yourself caring for or supporting others, emotionally or physically?
2. Are you craving more stability, routine, or predictability in your daily life?
3. Do you tend to overthink, worry, or get stuck in repetitive thought loops?
4. Do you sometimes feel emotionally heavy, overwhelmed, or burdened?
5. Are you struggling to balance giving to others with caring for yourself?

Just for today, I will let go of worry and trust the flow of life.

Physical & Energetic Clues

6. Do you experience digestive issues, bloating, or sluggishness?
7. Are you feeling ungrounded, tired, or mentally foggy?
8. Do you feel like your energy is leaking or constantly being drained?
9. Are you holding tension in your belly, thighs, or lower body?
10. Do you have difficulty saying "no" or setting boundaries with others?

Spiritual & Lifestyle Alignment

11. Do you feel disconnected from your body or find it hard to stay present?
12. Are you struggling with self-worth or feeling like you're "not enough"?
13. Do you crave home comforts, soothing rituals, or more time to rest?
14. Do you long to feel safe, held, and emotionally secure?
15. Are you more attuned to the energy of late summer, harvest, or nourishment?

Scoring

- **Mostly YES:** You are embodying the **Earth Archetype** right now. This is a time for grounding, nourishment, self-care, and healthy support. Focus on routine, rest, and emotional balance.

- **Mostly SOMETIMES:** Earth energy is present, but may be imbalanced. You may be overextending or resisting structure. Simplify and return to your center.
- **Mostly NO:** Earth may be underactive or blocked. You might feel scattered, unsupported, or mentally overwhelmed. Reconnect with your body and the energy of stability.

Your Earth Practices

To restore balance with this archetype:

- Reiki over the **Solar Plexus**, **abdomen**, **knees**, or **feet**
- Grounding foods, warm herbal teas, and earth-toned clothing
- Gentle routines, cozy environments, or massage
- Use grounding essential oils like patchouli, vetiver, or ginger
- Affirmation: *"I am grounded, nourished, and whole."*

Just for today, I will let go of worry and trust the flow of life.

Metal Archetype: The Sage / Spiritual Refiner

"I release what no longer serves. I return to essence."

The **Metal Element** governs clarity, breath, spiritual refinement, and letting go. As an archetype, the **Sage** or **Spiritual Refiner** represents your inner wisdom—your ability to **discern truth, release attachment, and honor what is sacred**. This is the energy of breath, minimalism, and higher alignment.

When this Archetype is in Balance:

- You feel spiritually connected and clear in thought and expression.
- You communicate with ease and authenticity.
- You're able to release the past and move forward with lightness.
- You honor rituals, sacred space, and simplicity.
- Your breath is calm, deep, and supportive.

When this Archetype is Out of Balance:

- You may hold onto grief, regret, or perfectionism.
- Feelings of sadness, detachment, or isolation may arise.
- You experience tension in the chest, shallow breathing, or frequent colds.
- There may be difficulty expressing emotions or making decisions.

- A tendency toward harsh self-judgment or spiritual disconnection may emerge.

The Reiki Wisdom of the Sage:

In Reiki, the Sage archetype clears what is no longer aligned— thoughts, emotions, energetic patterns, and even physical stagnation. It helps the practitioner become a **channel for truth and light**, not by force, but by creating space for transformation.

Metal-focused Reiki sessions often:

- Begin or end with **breath awareness**
- Include hand placements at the **Throat Chakra, lungs,** or **Third Eye**
- Incorporate crystals like selenite, clear quartz, or herkimer diamond
- Use essential oils like frankincense, eucalyptus, or sage
- Pair beautifully with guided release rituals or grief support

Affirmations of the Metal Archetype:

"I let go with love and grace."
"My truth flows clearly and peacefully."
"Grief is sacred—and so is release."
"I return to what matters most."

The **Sage / Spiritual Refiner** is the perfect archetype for Reiki sessions that involve closure, grief, clarity, or spiritual refinement. It reminds both client and practitioner that

Just for today, I will let go of worry and trust the flow of life.

healing doesn't always add—it often subtracts. It is through *letting go* that we remember who we truly are.

Are You Embodying the Metal Archetype?

The Sage / Spiritual Refiner

Answer the questions below with **Yes, Sometimes**, or **No**. This quiz will help you determine whether the **Metal Element**—the energy of breath, clarity, grief, and sacred release—is active in your life, and whether it's balanced or seeking healing.

Emotional & Mental Themes

1. Do you feel a strong desire to simplify, declutter, or let go of something (physically or emotionally)?
2. Are you currently processing grief, loss, or a major life transition?
3. Do you feel more introspective, quiet, or spiritually reflective than usual?
4. Are you finding it difficult to express your feelings, especially sadness or vulnerability?
5. Do you often hold yourself to very high (sometimes rigid) standards?

Physical & Energetic Clues

6. Are you experiencing tension in your chest, shallow breathing, or lung-related issues?
7. Do you feel dry, cold, or energetically "hollow"?
8. Are your shoulders or throat tight, especially when trying to speak or express?

9. Do you often feel like something is unresolved, but you can't quite name it?
10. Have you felt emotionally disconnected or isolated, even around others?

Spiritual & Energetic Alignment

11. Are you drawn to rituals, breathwork, or quiet spiritual practices?
12. Do you long to reconnect with a sense of purpose or inner truth?
13. Are you called to clear energetic attachments or toxic patterns from your life?
14. Do you feel sensitive to beauty, light, or symbolism—even in small moments?
15. Do you resonate with the energy of autumn, wind, stillness, or sacred release?

Scoring

- **Mostly YES:** You are embodying the **Metal Archetype**. This is a time for clarity, refinement, and sacred letting go. Honor grief, speak your truth gently, and create space for your spiritual essence to breathe.
- **Mostly SOMETIMES:** Metal energy is stirring within you. You may be moving through a transitional phase—allow space for breath, reflection, and slow release.
- **Mostly NO:** Metal may be repressed or dormant. You may be holding on too tightly, avoiding emotional expression, or disconnected from your inner wisdom. Invite in stillness and allow grief or clutter to gently move through.

Just for today, I will let go of worry and trust the flow of life.

Your Metal Practices

To embody this archetype more fully:

- Reiki on the **Throat, Third Eye, lungs**, or **shoulders**
- Practice breathwork or gentle vocal release
- Simplify your space or calendar; create sacred pauses
- Use frankincense, eucalyptus, or peppermint essential oils
- Work with selenite, clear quartz, or white stones
- Affirmation: *"I let go with grace. I breathe in clarity and peace."*

Chapter 11: The Seasons Within – A Year of Elemental Reiki

Seasonal Routines and Rituals

Healing in Rhythm with the Natural World

Nature doesn't rush, force, or cling—it flows through a **sacred rhythm of transformation** with grace. The Five Elements mirror this rhythm in every living thing, including your energy field. When you align your Reiki practice with the **seasons of the Earth**, you begin to recognize the seasons **within yourself**.

Each time of year holds unique gifts for healing, reflection, and growth. By adjusting your **routines and rituals** to the season, you attune your body, emotions, and energy field to the wisdom of the natural world. You don't just give Reiki— you **live Reiki**, in harmony with the elements all around and within you.

Just for today, I will let go of worry and trust the flow of life.

Spring (Wood Element) – Planting Intentions & Renewing Energy

- **Rituals:**
    - Cleanse and declutter your space (physical & energetic)
    - Begin a new Reiki project or learning path
    - Set clear intentions with New Moon or Equinox energy
- **Practice Focus:** Liver & Gallbladder meridians, Solar Plexus chakra
- **Reiki Themes:** Growth, clarity, courage, vision

Summer (Fire Element) – Expanding, Connecting & Shining Bright

- **Rituals:**
    - Host Reiki shares or heart-centered gatherings
    - Practice gratitude journaling under the Full Moon
    - Meditate outdoors and connect with sun/fire energy
- **Practice Focus:** Heart & Small Intestine meridians, Heart chakra
- **Reiki Themes:** Joy, passion, emotional balance, heart expression

Late Summer (Earth Element) – Grounding, Digesting & Centering

- **Rituals:**
    - Create nourishing meals and mindful eating rituals

- o Tend to your home altar or healing space
- o Reflect on the first half of the year—what's working? What's draining?
- **Practice Focus:** Spleen & Stomach meridians, Root & Solar Plexus chakras
- **Reiki Themes:** Nurturing, integration, simplicity, worry release

Autumn (Metal Element) – Letting Go & Refining Clarity

- **Rituals:**
  - o Create a letting-go ceremony (letters, leaves, breathwork)
  - o Purify your space with sage, sound, or Reiki symbols
  - o Focus on breathwork and silent meditations
- **Practice Focus:** Lung & Large Intestine meridians, Throat & Third Eye chakras
- **Reiki Themes:** Grief, clarity, refinement, boundaries

Winter (Water Element) – Resting, Dreaming & Replenishing

- **Rituals:**
  - o Practice longer Reiki self-treatments or deep rest meditations
  - o Journal your dreams and inner guidance
  - o Create space for silence, solitude, and spiritual reflection
- **Practice Focus:** Kidneys & Bladder meridians, Root & Sacral chakras
- **Reiki Themes:** Stillness, fear release, trust, energetic restoration

Just for today, I will let go of worry and trust the flow of life.

By honoring these rhythms, you deepen your practice and allow **seasonal wisdom to guide your intuition**, your sessions, and your own healing journey.

"To live in tune with nature is to live in tune with your soul."

Monthly Journaling Prompts

Tracking Energy, Emotions & Elemental Alignment Through the Year

As the seasons shift outside, they awaken subtle shifts within. Journaling with the elements helps you become more **attuned to the rhythms of your own energy**, revealing patterns, blocks, insights, and transformations. These monthly prompts are designed to complement your Reiki practice, self-care rituals, and personal growth journey.

You can use them at the start of each month, moon cycle, or as part of your post-Reiki reflections.

Spring (Wood Element – March, April, May)

- Where in my life do I feel ready to grow or take action?
- What frustration or tension am I ready to release?
- What is the vision I hold for the next season of my life?
- What would I do if I trusted my direction completely?
- How can I channel anger into positive movement?

Summer (Fire Element – June, July, August)

- What lights me up right now? Where do I feel joy?
- Where am I overextending myself emotionally?
- How can I express love more freely (to myself or others)?

Just for today, I will let go of worry and trust the flow of life.

- Am I giving myself time to rest and receive, or am I burning out?
- What does true emotional balance look like for me?

Late Summer (Earth Element – August, September)

- What am I currently digesting—emotionally, mentally, spiritually?
- Where do I feel worry or mental clutter showing up in my body?
- How can I nurture myself the way I nurture others?
- What practices help me feel grounded and centered?
- What do I need to simplify in my life right now?

Autumn (Metal Element – October, November)

- What am I ready to let go of?
- What lesson did I learn from what I've lost?
- Where am I holding on out of fear or habit?
- What do I value most deeply in my life right now?
- What clarity is trying to emerge from within?

Winter (Water Element – December, January, February)

- What fear or resistance is keeping me from being still?
- What dreams or inner guidance are surfacing in my quiet moments?
- How do I restore my energy when the world asks for more than I can give?
- Where in my life do I need more flow?
- What would trusting the unknown feel like?

Use these prompts in your **Elemental Reiki Journal**, client sessions, or group rituals. Over time, they become **a map of your inner seasons**—showing how you grow, let go, and return to yourself again and again.

"Each month is a mirror. Each season, a sacred invitation to listen more deeply to your soul."

Solstice and Equinox Reiki Rituals

Honoring the Turning Points of Light and Energy

The **Solstices and Equinoxes** mark powerful thresholds in the Earth's journey—moments when **light, dark, and energy are rebalanced**. These natural turning points offer ideal opportunities for Reiki practitioners to deepen healing work, release old energies, and set new intentions in alignment with the rhythm of the Earth.

Each event corresponds to one or more of the **Five Elements**, making them perfect anchors for **elemental Reiki rituals** that invite transformation, clarity, and energetic renewal.

You can practice these rituals for yourself, offer them as **seasonal ceremonies for clients**, or host **community healing circles**.

Spring Equinox (Wood Element)

Date: Around March 20 / Theme: Renewal, Balance, Intention

This is a time of **rebirth and forward motion**. Day and night are equal, symbolizing the balance between vision and grounded action.
Ritual Ideas:

- Reiki intention-setting ceremony for new goals or projects
- Use green candles, plants, or flower petals around the session space

- Offer journaling prompts for growth: *What am I ready to begin?*
- Focus Reiki on the **Solar Plexus, Liver/Gallbladder meridians**, and feet (for rooted growth)

Summer Solstice (Fire Element)

Date: Around June 21 | Theme: Radiance, Expansion, Expression

The longest day of the year—the sun at its peak. This is a celebration of **joy, vitality, and full creative bloom**.
Ritual Ideas:

- Open your session with gratitude and heart-based affirmations
- Work with the **Heart Chakra** and solar energy during Reiki
- Use gold, red, or pink cloths, and diffuse **rose or citrus oils**
- Invite your client to speak an intention aloud to "charge" it with light
- Finish with Reiki to the Third Eye and grounding to help integrate

Autumn Equinox (Metal + Earth Elements)

Date: Around September 22 | Theme: Reflection, Letting Go, Harvest

Another moment of balance—equal light and dark—but now the energy shifts inward. This is a time to **harvest wisdom**

Just for today, I will let go of worry and trust the flow of life.

and **begin releasing**.
Ritual Ideas:

- Offer Reiki focused on the **Lungs**, **Large Intestine**, and **Throat Chakra**
- Write "what no longer serves" on leaves or paper and burn or bury them
- Use white, grey, or earthy tones in the healing space
- Invite breathwork, stillness, and silence into the session
- End with an affirmation like: *"I release with grace. I keep only what is true."*

Winter Solstice (Water Element)

Date: Around December 21 / Theme: Stillness, Trust, Deep Renewal

The longest night of the year. The return of light begins, but in the darkness, we are asked to **rest, reflect, and dream**.
Ritual Ideas:

- Offer a deeply still Reiki session focusing on the **Root & Sacral Chakras**, **Kidneys**, and emotional safety
- Use candlelight, soft blankets, and grounding oils like vetiver or sandalwood
- Guide a meditation or visualization: *"What is gestating in the dark?"*
- Invite your client to silently hold a dream or intention during the session
- Close with a cup of warm tea or a grounding practice

These seasonal rituals deepen the **spiritual and energetic container** of your Reiki sessions. They allow your practice to become part of the Earth's sacred rhythm—reminding both you and your clients that healing is a **cyclical journey, not a linear path**.

"When we heal in rhythm with the Earth, we move in harmony with the divine."

Just for today, I will let go of worry and trust the flow of life.

Aligning Your Energy Healing Practice with Nature's Rhythms

Becoming a Practitioner in Tune with the Earth's Pulse

Nature is your first teacher. Before the books, the symbols, the trainings—there was the sun rising and setting, the moon cycling through its phases, the tide pulling in and out, and the seasons unfolding without effort.

When you align your energy healing practice with **nature's rhythms**, your work becomes not just more powerful—it becomes more **resonant, sustainable, and intuitive**. You're no longer working against the current. You're flowing with the larger energy field of life.

Why Seasonal Alignment Matters in Reiki

- Your **clients are influenced** by the same energetic shifts happening in the Earth. By acknowledging seasonal themes, you validate their inner experience and offer deeper support.
- You become a **mirror of harmony**, modeling balance, awareness, and adaptation.
- Nature offers **built-in cycles for rest, release, growth, and celebration**—these can guide your personal and professional rhythm.

Ways to Align Your Practice with the Seasons

1. Structure Your Services Seasonally

Offer **season-specific Reiki sessions, workshops, or rituals**. For example:

- "Spring Detox + Visioning" (Wood)
- "Summer Heart Activation" (Fire)
- "Autumn Release & Realignment" (Metal)
- "Winter Rest & Reiki Reset" (Water)
- "Late Summer Nourish & Center" (Earth)

This helps clients **connect emotionally** with what they're experiencing and gives your offerings a natural structure.

2. Weave Seasonal Language into Your Practice

In client conversations, newsletters, social media posts, or guided meditations, speak to what the Earth is reflecting:

"As the leaves fall, what are you ready to release?"
"As winter draws us inward, how are you restoring your energy?"

This creates a **relatable, intuitive bridge** between energy healing and everyday life.

3. Adjust Your Self-Care and Reiki Flow

- In **Spring**, rise earlier, practice creative Reiki flows, and focus on vision.
- In **Summer**, stay hydrated, slow your pace, and prioritize emotional balance.

Just for today, I will let go of worry and trust the flow of life.

- In **Autumn**, simplify your schedule and focus on cleansing your space.
- In **Winter**, go inward—longer meditations, journaling, and gentler sessions.
- In **Late Summer**, nourish your body and reinforce your energetic boundaries.

Let your Reiki practice evolve with the world around you. This is the **path of elemental mastery**—not perfection, but presence.

"You are not separate from the seasons. You are the seasons. Your healing work flows through their wisdom, and your spirit remembers its rhythm."

Using the Seasons Within for Your Clients

How Reiki Practitioners Can Align Healing with the Rhythms of Nature

As a Reiki practitioner, your role is not only to facilitate healing but to **guide clients into deeper self-awareness and connection**—both to their inner landscape and to the natural cycles that support it. The elemental and seasonal framework in this chapter gives you a **powerful, intuitive structure** to work with clients all year long.

Here's how to use this seasonal wisdom in your Reiki practice:

1. Elemental Assessment During Intakes

Begin by identifying which element is most active or imbalanced in your client. Consider:

- What season are you currently in—and how is your client responding to it?
- Which emotions or physical symptoms are present? (e.g., grief in autumn, anxiety in summer)
- Which monthly prompt resonates with what they're experiencing?

You can gently introduce these reflections as part of your client intake form, consultation, or post-session discussion.

Just for today, I will let go of worry and trust the flow of life.

2. Offer Journaling Prompts as Homework or Reflection

At the end of a Reiki session, offer one or two **seasonal journaling prompts** (from this chapter) that match the client's current emotional or energetic needs. These can deepen integration and empower clients to continue their healing between sessions.

For example:

"Since we worked on your Heart and Fire element today, try reflecting on: *What lights me up right now? Where do I feel joy?*"

You can also keep **printable cards or a seasonal journal page** in your treatment space to hand out or email afterward.

3. Tailor Reiki Techniques to Seasonal Energy

Each season invites a different Reiki approach:

- **Spring:** More active energy work, focus on Solar Plexus and flow
- **Summer:** Calming heart-centered sessions, cooling energy
- **Late Summer:** Grounding hand positions, digestive focus
- **Autumn:** Breathwork, grief release, clarity techniques
- **Winter:** Deep stillness, Root Chakra focus, energy replenishment

These rhythms help your clients **harmonize with what nature is already offering them**—making the healing more sustainable and embodied.

4. Create Seasonal Packages or Ritual Sessions

You can even structure your offerings around the elements and seasons:

- **"Spring Renewal Session"** for clarity and new beginnings
- **"Summer Heart Healing"** to release emotional overwhelm
- **"Autumn Release + Clarity"** to let go and restore breath
- **"Winter Restorative Reiki"** for nervous system reset and energetic nourishment

This not only supports your clients—it also expands your practice with **intuitive structure and seasonal variety**.

"When you align your Reiki sessions with the seasons, you help your clients do more than heal. You help them remember that they are part of something greater—cyclical, sacred, and whole."

Elemental Chart Quick Reference

Element	Primary Chakra(s)	Emotional Themes	Common Symptoms (Energetic/Physical)	Affirmations
Water	Root & Sacral	Fear, insecurity, trust	Fatigue, fear, adrenal burnout, kidney/bladder imbalance	"I am safe." "I trust the flow." "Stillness restores me."
Wood	Solar Plexus	Anger, frustration, direction	Tension in jaw/shoulders, headaches, liver/gallbladder congestion	"I release what holds me back." "I grow with purpose."
Fire	Heart	Joy, love, overwhelm	Anxiety, insomnia, emotional highs/lows, heart palpitations	"My heart is calm." "I radiate joy." "I am safe to feel."
Earth	Root & Solar Plexus	Worry, overthinking, support	Digestive issues, mental fatigue, heaviness, lack of motivation	"I am grounded." "I nourish myself." "I am enough."
Metal	Throat & Third Eye	Grief, clarity, letting go	Lung/chest tightness, skin issues, sadness, elimination imbalance	"I release with love." "I breathe in clarity." "I let go."

How to Use This Chart:

- Quickly reference before or during sessions to choose hand positions, affirmations, or tools
- Use with the **Reiki + Five Element Intake Form** to identify areas of focus
- Pair with seasonal care and journaling prompts to offer **element-specific guidance**
- Integrate into teaching materials, workshops, or client takeaway sheets

Just for today, I will let go of worry and trust the flow of life.

Seasonal Care Tracker

A Year of Elemental Self-Awareness

Use this tracker to tune into your **physical, emotional, and energetic shifts** throughout the seasons. It helps identify patterns, imbalances, or breakthroughs related to each element, allowing you to adjust your **Reiki self-care**, rituals, or session focus accordingly.

You can print one for each season, or use the full set as a **yearlong wellness journal companion**.

Spring – Wood Element (March, April, May)

- **Keywords:** Growth, movement, clarity, frustration, new beginnings
- How's my energy today?

  _____

- What am I ready to grow or change?

  _____

- Where do I feel tension or resistance in my body?

  _____

- Elemental self-care this week:

  _____

Summer – Fire Element (June, July, August)

- **Keywords:** Joy, passion, connection, emotional balance, expression
- How do I feel emotionally?

  _____

- What brings me joy right now?

  _____

- Am I resting enough between bursts of energy?

  _____

- Elemental self-care this week:

  _____

Late Summer – Earth Element (August, September)

- **Keywords:** Grounding, digestion, worry, nourishment, support
- What am I overthinking or holding onto?

  _____

- How do I feel after meals or Reiki sessions?

  _____

- Where do I need more support or stability?

  _____

- Elemental self-care this week:

  _____

Just for today, I will let go of worry and trust the flow of life.

Autumn – Metal Element (October, November)

- **Keywords:** Clarity, grief, breath, letting go, refinement
- What am I ready to release?

_____

- What emotion is sitting just beneath the surface?

_____

- Is my environment helping or hindering my clarity?

_____

- Elemental self-care this week:

_____

Winter – Water Element (December, January, February)

- **Keywords:** Stillness, fear, trust, reflection, replenishment
- How rested do I feel?

_____

- What am I afraid to feel or explore?

_____

- What's quietly trying to emerge from within me?

_____

- Elemental self-care this week:

_____

Tip: Use this tracker with monthly journaling prompts or during Reiki self-treatments to reflect on your alignment with the Five Elements. You can also ask clients to bring it back for follow-up discussions.

Reiki + Five Element Intake Form

Reiki + Five Element Intake Form

Client Self-Assessment for Elemental Balance

Client Name: _____

Date: _____

Practitioner: _____

Part 1: General Well-being

1. What brings you in for a Reiki session today?

   _____

2. Are there specific physical concerns you'd like support with?

   _____

3. Are there emotional patterns or stressors currently affecting your well-being?

   _____

4. How would you describe your current energy levels?
   ☐ Low ☐ Balanced ☐ Overactive ☐ Up and down

Part 2: Elemental Self-Check

Please check any experiences or symptoms you're currently feeling or noticing:

Just for today, I will let go of worry and trust the flow of life.

Water (Winter / Kidneys & Bladder / Root & Sacral)

- ☐ Fear or anxiety
- ☐ Lower back/kidney issues
- ☐ Fatigue or burnout
- ☐ Feeling withdrawn or emotionally numb
- ☐ Difficulty trusting or resting

Wood (Spring / Liver & Gallbladder / Solar Plexus)

- ☐ Frustration or irritability
- ☐ Jaw tension, headaches
- ☐ Feeling stuck or indecisive
- ☐ Digestive imbalance
- ☐ Needing direction or motivation

Fire (Summer / Heart & Small Intestine / Heart Chakra)

- ☐ Anxiety or emotional highs/lows
- ☐ Sleep disturbances or restlessness
- ☐ Difficulty expressing emotions
- ☐ Burnout or overextension
- ☐ Desire for deeper connection or joy

Earth (Late Summer / Spleen & Stomach / Root & Solar Plexus)

- ☐ Worry or overthinking
- ☐ Feeling ungrounded or heavy
- ☐ Digestive issues or cravings
- ☐ Giving too much to others
- ☐ Difficulty centering or focusing

Metal (Autumn / Lungs & Large Intestine / Throat & Third Eye)

- ☐ Grief or difficulty letting go
- ☐ Chest tightness or shallow breathing
- ☐ Skin or elimination issues
- ☐ Emotional flatness or spiritual disconnection
- ☐ Desire for clarity and simplicity

Part 3: Intentions & Support

1. What is your intention or hope for this session?

   _____

2. Is there a particular element, chakra, or emotion you'd like to explore or support?

   _____

3. How comfortable are you with receiving Reiki or energy work?
   ☐ First time ☐ Some experience ☐ Regular practice

Practitioner Note: Use this form to guide your **session layout, affirmations, and aftercare suggestions**. Over time, this intake can become part of a client's **seasonal or elemental healing journey**.

Just for today, I will let go of worry and trust the flow of life.

Final Integration Ritual: A Sacred Elemental Alignment

Bringing the Five Elements into Harmony Within

This ritual is a sacred closing to your journey through the Five Elements and Reiki energy. It is not a performance—it is a **personal attunement**, a spiritual remembering. This is your invitation to become the vessel through which elemental harmony flows.

This ritual can be performed:

- As a personal ceremony
- Before beginning Elemental Reiki sessions with clients
- At the turning of a season or significant life shift
- After completing the course, book, or attunement process

You are not simply learning the elements—you are becoming them.
This ritual opens the gateway to live, breathe, and channel them in balance.

Preparation

- Find a quiet, comfortable space where you won't be disturbed.
- Optional: Light five candles (one for each element— blue, green, red, yellow, white/gray) or place five symbolic objects around you.

- You may choose to play soft elemental music, chimes, or nature sounds.

Sit comfortably with your spine aligned and your hands resting gently on your lap or heart. Take several deep, slow breaths to center.

1. Call in the Earth Element

Whisper or speak aloud:

"I call in the grounding energy of Earth.
I am rooted, nourished, and supported."

Place hands on your lower belly or feet.
Visualize deep roots growing from your body into the soil.
Feel the Earth holding you, solid and steady.

Breathe deeply into your body. Feel yourself becoming fully present.

2. Call in the Water Element

Whisper or speak aloud:

"I call in the flowing energy of Water.
I am in tune with my emotions, and I trust the rhythm of life."

Place hands over the sacral chakra or kidneys.
Visualize a flowing river moving through you, clearing stagnant energy, softening resistance, restoring flow.

Let your breath move like a wave—gentle, circular, calm.

Just for today, I will let go of worry and trust the flow of life.

3. Call in the Wood Element

Whisper or speak aloud:

"I call in the energy of Wood.
I grow with purpose, and I move forward with clarity."

Place hands on the Solar Plexus or heart.
Visualize yourself as a strong tree—roots in the earth,
branches rising. Feel creative energy rise through your spine.
Let vision and direction return.

Breathe with strength and intention.

4. Call in the Fire Element

Whisper or speak aloud:

"I call in the radiant energy of Fire.
I shine with joy, love, and purpose."

Place hands on your Heart Chakra or gently over your eyes.
Visualize a golden flame glowing in your chest. Let it grow
brighter. Feel joy, passion, and love awaken

Smile softly. Let your breath warm and open you.

5. Call in the Metal Element

Whisper or speak aloud:

"I call in the breath of Metal.
I release what no longer serves. I return to essence."

Place hands on your throat or lightly over the crown.
Visualize a silver mist cleansing you. Let go of tension, doubt, and old attachments. Feel your breath as sacred.

Exhale completely. Feel the spaciousness of your spirit.

Final Alignment: Embody the Circle

Bring your hands together in prayer position at your heart.
Feel the five elements spiraling in harmony within you:
Earth grounding you...
Water flowing through you...
Wood rising with purpose...
Fire shining from your heart...
Metal clearing and refining your spirit.

Stay here for several breaths.
Feel the integration. Feel the stillness. Feel the wholeness.

Closing Affirmation:

"I am the vessel of balance.
The Five Elements live within me.
I am aligned with nature, purpose, and spirit.
I am ready to offer healing in harmony."

Just for today, I will let go of worry and trust the flow of life.

Suggested Meditations for Elemental Reiki Practice

Short Guided Practices for Inner Balance & Energetic Alignment

Each of the following meditations aligns with one of the Five Elements. They are designed to be simple, soothing, and supportive—ideal for use before or after Reiki, during seasonal rituals, or as a personal practice to harmonize mind, body, and spirit.

You may guide these meditations aloud for clients, share them as written scripts, or adapt them into audio tracks for your Elemental Reiki program.

Water Meditation – "The Still Lake"

Focus: Trust, emotional flow, and rest

Visualize yourself standing before a still, crystal-clear lake. With every breath in, the surface becomes smoother. With every exhale, you let go of tension. Feel yourself become one with the water—deep, reflective, calm. Say silently: *"I am safe. I trust the stillness. I flow with life."*

Use before Reiki sessions that involve Root or Sacral Chakra healing, fear, or exhaustion.

Wood Meditation – "The Tree Within"

Focus: Growth, clarity, and direction

Imagine yourself as a young tree rooted firmly into the Earth. You feel energy rising through your trunk, up through your spine, and out through your arms like branches stretching to the sky. The wind moves gently around you, but you remain flexible and grounded. Say: *"I rise with purpose. I grow with ease."*

Ideal for supporting clients with decision-making, anger release, or creative stagnation.

Fire Meditation – "Heart Flame"

Focus: Joy, expression, emotional balance

Place your hand over your heart and imagine a soft golden flame glowing within. This flame is your inner joy, steady and warm. With each breath, it expands—not wildly, but gently—illuminating your chest, then your body, then your aura. Say: *"I shine from within. My heart is light and open."*

Use this meditation to center during heart-based Reiki sessions or during emotional overwhelm.

Just for today, I will let go of worry and trust the flow of life.

Earth Meditation – "Center of the Mountain"

Focus: Grounding, nourishment, inner stability

Visualize yourself sitting within the belly of a great mountain. Around you is calm, dark earth—protective and steady. You feel the pulse of the Earth below you, like a soft drumbeat syncing with your breath. Say: *"I am grounded. I am supported. I am enough."*

Perfect for worry, overthinking, digestive issues, or those needing reassurance and self-connection.

Metal Meditation – "The Breath of Letting Go"

Focus: Grief release, clarity, spiritual refinement

Imagine standing in an open field on an autumn morning. You take a deep breath in through your nose—cool, crisp air filling your lungs. As you exhale, visualize a mist of old energy, grief, or heaviness leaving your body. You are lighter. Say: *"I let go with grace. I breathe in peace. I remember who I am."*

Supportive for sessions involving the Lungs, grief work, throat expression, or spiritual clarity.

Practitioner Journal Pages

A Reflection Companion for Elemental Reiki Sessions

These pages are for **your personal practice**—to deepen your awareness, strengthen your intuition, and refine your approach as an Elemental Reiki Practitioner. Use them after client sessions, during your self-treatments, or at the start of each season to explore your energetic rhythm and growth.

You can print one page per session or use them in a dedicated Elemental Reiki journal.

Session Reflection Page (Client or Self-Treatment)

Date: _____

Season: _____

Element(s) in Focus:

_____

Client Name (or Self):

_____

Presenting Issue or Focus:

_____

Notable Emotions or Energetic Patterns Observed:

_____

Chakras or Meridians Engaged:

_____

Just for today, I will let go of worry and trust the flow of life.

Tools Used (Crystals, Oils, Sound, Visualization):

_____

Affirmations or Insights Shared:

_____

Notable Shifts or Observations During Session:

_____

Aftercare Recommendations Given (if any):

_____

Follow-up Needed? ☐ Yes ☐ No
If yes, suggested timeline: _____

_____

Seasonal Reflection Page (Quarterly Practice Review)

Current Season:

_____

Elemental Energy This Season Feels:
☐ Balanced   ☐ Deficient   ☐ Excessive   ☐ Unclear

Themes Emerging in My Clients or Myself:

_____

Where am I personally being called to grow or release?

_____

How am I honoring this season in my Reiki work and life?

_____

Tools or Rituals I'm drawn to right now:

_____

Affirmation for this season:

_____

_____

"The more you listen, the more you'll feel. The more you feel, the more you'll know. And the more you know, the deeper your healing work becomes."

Just for today, I will let go of worry and trust the flow of life.

Returning to the Rhythm Within

As you reach the end of this book, know that you are not reaching an end at all—but rather a return. A return to the part of you that is always in rhythm with the Earth. A return to your breath, your body, your energy. A return to the deep, wise knowing that **healing isn't something we chase— it's something we remember**.

Reiki is the light that flows through all living things. The Five Elements are the sacred language that light speaks through the world around and within you. When these two powerful systems meet, healing becomes not just possible—it becomes natural.

Through the changing seasons, shifting emotions, and cycles of balance and imbalance, you now have tools, insights, and rituals that can help you align, release, nourish, and grow. Whether you are working with clients or journeying through your own healing, the elements will always be there to **mirror what needs attention, offer guidance, and hold space for transformation.**

You have learned how to:

- Listen to energy through both feeling and form.
- Partner with nature to support body, mind, and spirit.
- Use Reiki not only as a healing technique, but as a way of **living in harmony**.

This is the gift of Elemental Reiki: it doesn't separate the mystical from the everyday. It brings the sacred into the soil, into the breath, into your hands—and reminds you that you are never alone on your healing path.

So let this be your invitation:
To walk with the seasons.
To trust your inner tides.
To be the stillness of winter, the fire of summer, the tree growing in spring, and the leaves letting go in fall.
To offer healing with integrity, presence, and love.

And most of all—
To remember that **you are nature.**
You are energy.
You are Reiki.
And you are ready.

With light, balance, and deep gratitude,
Dr. Constance Santego
Grand Reiki Master, Elemental Guide, and Keeper of Nature's Wisdom

Just for today, I will let go of worry and trust the flow of life.

A Mantra for Elemental Harmony

May the Water within you flow with grace,
washing away fear,
and guiding you into trust.

May the Wood within you rise strong,
rooted in purpose,
stretching always toward your truth.

May the Fire within you burn steady and kind,
warming your heart,
and igniting your joy.

May the Earth within you hold you gently,
offering nourishment,
and reminding you that you are enough.

May the Metal within you shine bright and clear,
cutting through illusion,
and helping you let go with grace.

And may Reiki—pure light, pure love —
move through your hands,
your heart,
your voice,
and your life...

as you become a vessel
for balance, healing, and wholeness—
for yourself,
and for the world. **And so it is.**

Five Element Attunement Meditation

(Part One)

"The Elemental Awakening"

This meditation is intended to be spoken aloud by the Reiki Master or listened to as an audio recording. It brings the student into deep relaxation, energetic readiness, and connection to the Five Elemental Guides who will accompany them in their Reiki journey.

Introduction: Deep Relaxation

(Adapted to blend the traditional with the elemental)

"Close your eyes... and begin to relax your body.
Take a long, slow breath... all the way down to the base of your spine.
Now let it go... and feel yourself beginning to settle.
Feel your awareness gather gently behind your eyes...
Let your eyelids grow heavier... your breath slower...
Relax your jaw, your neck, your shoulders...
Let the warmth of peace move down through your chest, your stomach, your hips...
Relax your thighs, your knees... all the way down to your toes.

Now take another breath in—and as you exhale, let go of everything that is not needed.
Let your mind become soft... open... still.

Earth Element – The Foundation

Just for today, I will let go of worry and trust the flow of life.

"I call in the energy of **Earth**—the stabilizer, the nurturer, the root."

Visualize a golden brown light forming beneath you. It glows from the center of the Earth and rises to meet your body.
Let this light enter through your **feet**, rising to your knees, hips, and base of your spine.
Feel it anchoring you into the Earth… steady, grounded, supported.

"I am safe. I am held. I belong."

Water Element – The Flow

"I call in the energy of **Water**—the deep listener, the dreamer, the healer."

Now a shimmering **blue light** begins to flow through your **sacral center and lower back**.
This is the energy of your emotions, intuition, and inner flow.
Feel it washing over you, dissolving resistance, softening your breath, awakening peace.

"I trust the flow. I feel deeply. I move with grace."

Wood Element – The Vision

"I call in the energy of **Wood**—the visionary, the pathfinder, the force of growth."

A vibrant **green light** begins to rise from the Earth, weaving through your **solar plexus** and spine.
This is your power to grow, to move forward, to take aligned

action.
Feel it like the strength of a tree growing within you—
resilient, flexible, and alive.

"I grow with clarity. I rise with purpose."

Fire Element – The Heart Flame

"I call in the energy of **Fire**—the lover, the joyful creator, the
heart's radiance."

A warm, glowing **red and gold light** blossoms in your **heart
center**.
Feel it expanding outward, opening your chest, your breath,
and your joy.
Let this light warm your hands, your voice, your spirit.

"My heart is open. I create with love. I shine my light freely."

Metal Element – The Breath of Spirit

"I call in the energy of **Metal**—the sage, the refiner, the
breath of truth."

A clear, silvery-white light begins to pour in from above your
head, gently touching your **throat, third eye, and crown**.
This is the energy of letting go, of clarity, of sacred
connection.
Feel it clearing your thoughts, your lungs, your spiritual
channel.
With each breath, release... and return to your essence.

"I let go with grace. I breathe in truth. I am clear."

Just for today, I will let go of worry and trust the flow of life.

Integration: The Elemental Spiral

Now, see all five lights—Earth, Water, Wood, Fire, Metal—
swirling gently through your body in perfect harmony.
They spiral through your chakras, weaving together like
threads of light, uniting Heaven and Earth within you.

You are now aligned with the Five Sacred Elements.
You are a channel for healing.
You are ready to be attuned.

*At this point, the Master would begin the physical
attunement process:*

1. Student holds their **Hui Yin point** and enters receptive
    stillness.
2. Master opens the **Crown Chakra** with the Raku
    symbol.
3. Master draws **Choku Rei** into the crown, heart, and
    palms.
4. Student takes a **Kidney Breath** to circulate energy
    through the microcosmic orbit.
5. Crown is sealed with **Raku** again.

Part Two: Awakening the Elemental Guides

You now begin to sense the presence of five guides—each a
spirit of one of the elements.
They stand around you, forming a sacred circle. You may see,
hear, or feel them in your own unique way.
They are here to walk with you, teach you, and amplify your
healing gifts.

- Earth stands behind you, strong and unwavering.
- Water flows to your left, soothing and silent.
- Wood grows to your right, tall and vibrant.
- Fire rises before you, bold and warm.
- Metal floats above, light as air, sharp as crystal.

They place their hands upon your energetic field—and with a shared breath, they seal your Elemental Reiki alignment.

Final Words

Repeat silently or aloud:

"I am a vessel of balance and harmony.
The Five Elements live within me.
I now carry the wisdom of nature through Reiki.
With love, light, and service—I begin."

Breathe deeply. Slowly return to your body.
Open your eyes when ready.
You are attuned.
You are whole.

Just for today, I will let go of worry and trust the flow of life.

Glossary

This glossary provides a quick reference for key terms, concepts, symbols, and techniques used in Reiki practice, including details from all three levels of Reiki (Shoden, Okuden, and Shinpiden). It serves as a comprehensive guide to help you deepen your understanding and apply Reiki principles effectively, particularly when working with joints and energy pathways.

A

Alignment – The balanced flow of energy through the chakras, meridians, and nadis. Proper alignment supports emotional, physical, and spiritual health.

Ajna Chakra – The Third Eye Chakra, located between the eyebrows. Governs intuition, perception, and insight.

Anahata Chakra – The Heart Chakra, located in the center of the chest. Governs love, compassion, and emotional balance.

Attunement – A sacred process in which a Reiki Master transfers the ability to channel Reiki energy to a student. Attunements are given during Reiki Level 1, 2, and 3 training.

Auric Field (Aura) – The energetic field surrounding the body. It consists of multiple layers connected to the chakras and reflects emotional, mental, physical, and spiritual health.

B

Balance – A state where energy flows freely through the body without blockage or resistance. Reiki helps restore balance at the physical, emotional, and spiritual levels.

Breathwork – Techniques that use conscious breathing to direct and enhance the flow of energy through the body.

C

Chakra – Spinning energy centers located along the central axis of the body. There are seven primary chakras and numerous secondary chakras located in the joints and extremities.

Cho Ku Rei – The Power Symbol. Used to increase the flow of Reiki energy, clear blockages, and activate protection.

- Meaning: "Place the power of the universe here."
- Application: Increases power, activates energy flow, and grounds the practitioner.

Cleansing – The process of releasing stagnant or blocked energy from the body or energetic field through Reiki or other energetic practices.

Conscious Intention – Focusing mental and spiritual energy on a specific outcome or goal during a Reiki session.

Crossroad (Energetic) – A point where multiple energy pathways (chakras, meridians, nadis) intersect. Joints often serve as energetic crossroads.

Just for today, I will let go of worry and trust the flow of life.

Crown Chakra (Sahasrara) – The seventh chakra, located at the top of the head. Governs spiritual connection and enlightenment.

D

Dai Ko Myo – The Master Symbol. Used in Reiki Level 3 for spiritual awakening, enlightenment, and deeper healing.

- Meaning: "The Great Shining Light."
- Application: Used to heal the soul and promote spiritual growth.

Distance Healing – Sending Reiki energy to a person, situation, or event across time and space using the symbol Hon Sha Ze Sho Nen.

E

Emotional Blockage – Stored emotional trauma or resistance that restricts the flow of energy through the chakras, nadis, or meridians.

Energy Field – The subtle energetic body surrounding and penetrating the physical body.

Energy Knot – A blockage in the flow of energy through a joint, chakra, or meridian.

F

Flow – The smooth movement of energy through the body's energy channels. Reiki restores flow when energy becomes stagnant.

Flexibility – The ability to adapt emotionally and spiritually, reflected physically in joint mobility.

H

Hand Positions – Specific placements of the hands on or above the body used to channel Reiki energy.

Heart Chakra – See **Anahata Chakra**

Hon Sha Ze Sho Nen – The Distance Symbol. Used to send Reiki across time and space.

- Meaning: "No past, no present, no future."
- Application: Used for healing events in the past, present, and future; also used for distance healing.

I

Ida Nadi – The left energy channel connected to feminine, cooling, and intuitive energy. Ida is linked to emotional balance and the parasympathetic nervous system.

Intuitive Reiki – Allowing Reiki to flow based on inner guidance rather than strict hand placements.

J

Joint – A physical and energetic intersection where multiple meridians and nadis meet. Joints store emotional patterns and influence energy flow throughout the body.

Just for today, I will let go of worry and trust the flow of life.

K

Ki – Life force energy that flows through the body's meridians and nadis. Reiki channels this energy for healing and balance.

Kundalini – Spiritual energy coiled at the base of the spine. When awakened, it rises through the chakras, leading to enlightenment.

L

Level 1 (Shoden) – The beginner level of Reiki where students learn:

- The history of Reiki.
- Basic hand positions for self-healing and healing others.
- The concept of ki (life force energy).

Level 2 (Okuden) – The practitioner level where students learn:

- Advanced hand positions.
- Emotional and mental healing.
- Reiki symbols (Cho Ku Rei, Sei He Ki, Hon Sha Ze Sho Nen).

Level 3 (Shinpiden) – The Master level where students learn:

- How to perform attunements.
- Spiritual healing and awakening.
- Master symbol (Dai Ko Myo).

M

Meridians – Pathways through which qi (life force energy) flows in the body. Used in Traditional Chinese Medicine and Reiki for energy balancing.

Mind-Body Connection – The relationship between emotional, mental, and physical health. Reiki works on all three levels simultaneously.

N

Nadi – Subtle energy channels through which prana (life force energy) flows. There are thousands of nadis, but the three primary nadis are Ida, Pingala, and Sushumna.

O

Okuden – See **Level 2**

P

Pingala Nadi – The right energy channel connected to masculine, heating, and active energy. Pingala is linked to physical energy and the sympathetic nervous system.

Prana – The life force energy that sustains all living beings.

R

Reiki – A Japanese healing technique that channels life force energy through the practitioner's hands into the recipient's body.

Just for today, I will let go of worry and trust the flow of life.

- Meaning: "Universal life force energy."

Root Chakra (Muladhara) – The first chakra, located at the base of the spine. Governs security, grounding, and survival.

S

Sahasrara – See **Crown Chakra**

Sei He Ki – The Emotional Symbol. Used to balance emotional and mental energy.

- Meaning: "God and man become one."
- Application: Used for emotional healing and removing mental patterns.

Shoden – See **Level 1**

Shinpiden – See **Level 3**

Solar Plexus Chakra (Manipura) – The third chakra, located at the upper abdomen. Governs confidence, personal power, and digestion.

Sushumna Nadi – The central energy channel that runs through the spine. When open, it allows spiritual awakening and the rise of kundalini energy.

T

Third Eye Chakra (Ajna) – See **Ajna Chakra**

Tsubo Points – Pressure points along the meridians that serve as access points for energy flow. Similar to secondary chakras.

U

Universal Energy – The source of Reiki energy, believed to be the creative force of the universe.

W

Wisdom Channel – Sushumna Nadi is often called the Wisdom Channel because it governs spiritual awareness and higher consciousness.

REI *(ray)*

Universal Life Energy
Spiritual Consciousness
All-Knowing

KI *(kee)*

Breath
Life Force
Vital Radiant Energy

Chokurei (Show Ku Ray)

Used for Physical Clearing.

Forward 7 is used for general or whole body, backward 7 is used for specific or small areas

Sei He Ki (Say Hey Key)

Used for Emotional Clearing and Mental Clearing

Hon Sha Ze Sho Nen, which is specifically associated with distant healing.

Just for today, I will let go of worry and trust the flow of life.

Companion Books

*More is taught about Energy healing, Chakras, and Reiki
in my book,*

"Secrets of a Healer – Magic of Reiki (Vol X)

Trade paperback ISBN: 978-1-7772220-0-0

eBook ISBN 978-1-7772220-1-7

By

DR. CONSTANCE SANTEGO

SECRETS OF A HEALER
VOL. XI
THE REIKI MASTER'S MANUAL

Trade paperback ISBN: 978-1-990062-34-6
eBook ISBN 978-1-990062-35-3

Just for today, I will let go of worry and trust the flow of life.

Angelic Lifestyle A Vibrant Lifestyle from a Grand Reiki Master

Trade paperback ISBN: 978-0-9952112-7-8

Angelic Lifestyle 42-Day Energy Cleanse

Trade paperback ISBN: 978-1-7770818-3-6
eBook ISBN 978-1-7770818-4-3

Just for today, I will let go of worry and trust the flow of life.

from my Novel Series,
"The Nine Spiritual Gifts Granted By Spirit"
Vol IV in the series, *"Miracles of a Soul"*

Soft Cover ISBN: 978-1-990062-12-4
eBook ISBN: 978-1-990062-13-1

BASED ON THE NINE SPIRITUAL GIFTS GRANTED BY SPIRIT

MIRACLES *of a* SOUL

A NOVEL
Lexi Constantine's Fifth Adventure
This Time with Archangel Hamied's Help
THE GIFT OF MIRACLES

CONSTANCE SANTEGO

Bibliography

The following sources include foundational texts on Reiki, Traditional Chinese Medicine, the Five Elements, energy healing, and the emotional-energetic connections within the body. This bibliography reflects a blend of classical Eastern wisdom, modern holistic practices, and practical healing guides. Together, these works provide a well-rounded and deeply rooted understanding of the elemental philosophy and energetic principles explored throughout *Reiki and the Five Elements: Balancing Energy Through Nature's Wisdom*.

Ando, Teruko. *The Art of Reiki: Healing with Universal Life Force Energy*. Tokyo: Ki Publications, 2012.

Beinfield, Harriet, and Korngold, Efrem. *Between Heaven and Earth: A Guide to Chinese Medicine*. New York: Ballantine Books, 1991.

Brennan, Barbara Ann. *Hands of Light: A Guide to Healing Through the Human Energy Field*. New York: Bantam, 1987.

Chopra, Deepak. *The Book of Secrets: Unlocking the Hidden Dimensions of Your Life*. New York: Harmony Books, 2004.

Gerber, Richard. *Vibrational Medicine: The #1 Handbook of Subtle-Energy Therapies*. Rochester, VT: Bear & Company, 2001.

Just for today, I will let go of worry and trust the flow of life.

Honervogt, Tanmaya. *The Power of Reiki: An Ancient Hands-On Healing Technique.* London: Hodder & Stoughton, 2000.

Kaptchuk, Ted J. *The Web That Has No Weaver: Understanding Chinese Medicine.* Chicago: Contemporary Books, 2000.

Miles, Pamela. *Reiki: A Comprehensive Guide.* New York: TarcherPerigee, 2006.

Santego, Constance. *Secrets of a Healer: Magic of Reiki.* Kelowna: Maximillian Enterprises, 2022.

Weil, Andrew. *Spontaneous Healing.* New York: Ballantine Books, 1995.

Zhi Gang Sha, Dr. *Soul Mind Body Medicine: A Complete Soul Healing System for Optimum Health and Vitality.* San Francisco: New World Library, 2006.

Note. Additional inspiration and knowledge for this book have been drawn from decades of hands-on practice, student case studies, and the oral teachings passed through the lineage of Reiki Masters and natural healing traditions.

Suggested Internet Resources

These online platforms offer valuable insights into Reiki, the Five Elements, holistic healing, emotional release, and the energetic systems of the body. They provide a mix of educational materials, practitioner tools, scientific research, spiritual guidance, and community support that complement the principles explored in *Reiki and the Five Elements: Balancing Energy Through Nature's Wisdom*. Whether you're seeking meditations, training, or inspiration, these trusted resources can guide you.

Reiki and Energy Healing

- **International Center for Reiki Training** –
  www.reiki.org
  One of the most comprehensive Reiki hubs, offering training programs, articles, and practitioner directories.
- **Reiki Rays** – www.reikirays.com
  A global Reiki community featuring techniques, hand positions, meditations, and practitioner insights.
- **Reiki Healing Association** –
  www.reikihealingassociation.com
  Membership-based organization with downloadable tools, certification support, and Reiki business tips.
- **The Reiki Alliance** – www.reikialliance.com
  Founded by students of Hawayo Takata, this site explores lineage, tradition, and global Reiki connection.

Just for today, I will let go of worry and trust the flow of life.

Elemental Wisdom, TCM & Chakra Systems

- **Sacred Centers (Anodea Judith)** –
  www.sacredcenters.com
  Extensive chakra training and books by a leading
  expert in energy psychology and body systems.
- **Chi Nei Tsang Institute** – www.chineitsang.com
  Focus on meridians, chi flow, and internal organ
  energy work from a Taoist healing perspective.
- **The Shift Network** – www.theshiftnetwork.com
  Offers holistic courses and summits on chakra
  balancing, seasonal energy healing, and intuition.

Emotional & Spiritual Healing

- **Louise Hay's Official Website** – www.louisehay.com
  Emotional affirmations, metaphysical insights, and
  mind-body healing techniques.
- **HeartMath Institute** – www.heartmath.org
  Science-backed tools for emotional coherence, stress
  relief, and energetic alignment.
- **EFT Tapping (EmoFree)** – www.emofree.com
  Learn the Emotional Freedom Technique to release
  stored emotional patterns through acupressure.
- **Dr. Joe Dispenza** – www.drjoedispenza.com
  Research and training on consciousness, energy
  medicine, brain states, and quantum healing.
- **Bessel van der Kolk** – www.besselvanderkolk.com
  Pioneer in trauma research and body-based healing.
  Author of *The Body Keeps the Score*.

Sound Healing, Breathwork & Visualization

- **Insight Timer** – www.insighttimer.com
  A free meditation app with Reiki-specific sessions, breathwork, and guided visualizations.
- **Sonic Bloom** – www.sonicbloom.com
  Sound healing resources, frequency charts, and vibrational therapy tools.
- **The Tuning Fork Shop** – www.tuningforkshop.com
  Sound tools for chakra and meridian balancing, including weighted forks and training.
- **Breathwork Alliance** – www.breathworkalliance.com
  A collective of breathwork professionals offering techniques for clearing energy blocks.

Books, Learning Platforms & Media

- **Goodreads** – www.goodreads.com
  Discover book lists, reviews, and reader favorites in energy healing, Reiki, and TCM.
- **Gaia** – www.gaia.com
  Spiritual documentaries, interviews, and courses on vibrational medicine and consciousness.
- **Coursera** – www.coursera.org
  University-level courses in mindfulness, TCM, and holistic health.
- **Open Path Collective** – www.openpathcollective.org
  Affordable access to integrative therapy, energy medicine practitioners, and online healing support.

Just for today, I will let go of worry and trust the flow of life.

Professional Reiki & Holistic Health Organizations

- **International Association of Reiki Professionals (IARP)** – www.iarp.org
  Networking, marketing tools, and global practitioner directories.
- **National Certification Board for Therapeutic Massage & Bodywork (NCBTMB)** – www.ncbtmb.org
  Continuing education provider for Reiki, bodyworkers, and holistic health professionals.
- **Holistic Health Practitioner Network** –
  www.holistichealthpractitioners.org
  Directory and resource hub for certified energy healers and alternative practitioners.

These online resources can support you in creating a Reiki practice that is **grounded, inspired, and aligned** with the elemental wisdom of nature. May they serve as companions on your ongoing healing journey.

Suggested Video Resources

Films & Documentaries on Energy, Emotion & Elemental Harmony

These video resources expand on the themes explored in this book—energy medicine, elemental balance, emotional patterns, and spiritual growth. Each film or documentary offers insight into the interconnected nature of the body, mind, and spirit. Whether you're a Reiki practitioner, energy healer, or seeker of deeper truths, these titles will inspire and awaken new levels of understanding.

Energy Healing & Vibrational Medicine

The Living Matrix (2009)
Explores the science behind energy healing, consciousness, and quantum biology. Features pioneers in holistic health and the human energy field.

E-Motion (2014)
Reveals how trapped emotions influence physical health and how releasing emotional energy can restore wellness. Perfect companion for elemental emotional healing.

Heal (2017)
A powerful documentary that investigates the connection between mindset, beliefs, and the body's ability to heal. Interviews with leading experts in energy medicine and psychology.

Frequency of Genius (2020)
Explores how sound, frequency, and vibration shape human

Just for today, I will let go of worry and trust the flow of life.

consciousness, health, and transformation. A great link to elemental sound healing practices.

Elemental Wisdom & Nature-Based Healing

Inner Worlds, Outer Worlds (2012)
A spiritual documentary exploring the sacred geometry, vibration, and consciousness that connect all life—bridging the microcosm and macrocosm, much like the Five Elements.

Fantastic Fungi (2019)
While focused on fungi, this film offers deep insight into Earth's natural intelligence, cycles, and the energetic symbiosis of life—wonderful inspiration for Earth element practices.

The Secret Life of Plants (1979)
A classic exploring the emotional and energetic sensitivity of plants—demonstrating energy flow and intuitive connection in the natural world.

Mind-Body-Spirit Connection

What the Bleep Do We Know!? (2004)
A metaphysical journey through quantum physics, consciousness, and the power of belief to reshape our reality. Offers a foundational perspective for Reiki and energetic work.

The Power of the Heart (2014)
Explores how the heart is more than a physical organ—it's a source of intuition, healing, and energetic guidance. Deeply relevant to the Fire element and heart-based Reiki sessions.

You Can Heal Your Life (2007)
Based on Louise Hay's teachings, this film bridges affirmations, energy patterns, and healing. A visual guide to emotional clearing and spiritual self-awareness.

Spiritual Growth, Stillness & Inner Wisdom

The Shift (2009, featuring Dr. Wayne Dyer)
Explores the transition from ambition to meaning, aligning perfectly with the Metal and Water elements' call to let go and listen inwardly.

Awake: The Life of Yogananda (2014)
Follows the life of Paramahansa Yogananda, a pioneer in bringing meditation and energy practices to the West. Inspires spiritual devotion and disciplined energy flow.

Samadhi (2017)
An immersive journey into the nature of consciousness and awakening. A beautiful complement to the deeper states of Reiki meditation and inner elemental alignment.

These video resources can be used for personal reflection, continuing education, Reiki classes, or seasonal workshops. They serve as powerful tools to **see, feel, and understand energy in motion**—and to remember the deeper story we're all a part of.

Just for today, I will let go of worry and trust the flow of life.

Message From The Author

The Five Elements are more than philosophical ideas — they are living energies that shape the world around us and move within us. Just like the seasons, we too cycle through phases of growth, release, stillness, joy, and reflection. What continues to amaze me about Reiki is how gracefully it mirrors these cycles — gently guiding energy back into flow where it has become stuck or forgotten.

When I began working with Reiki through the lens of elemental wisdom, everything deepened. Clients who were feeling overwhelmed in the summer found clarity by reconnecting with Fire. Those lost in grief during autumn softened as Metal helped them let go. Winter's stillness taught the beauty of rest and trust through Water, while Earth reminded us to ground and nourish. Wood called us to grow again.

The body is always speaking through these elemental imbalances — not just with pain or fatigue, but with emotions like worry, anger, fear, or the inability to move forward. Reiki doesn't just soothe the symptoms; it **translates the energy**, helping you understand where healing is needed and how to gently restore balance.

This book was born from my desire to give practitioners a more intuitive, nature-based map for healing — one that blends the structure of Traditional Chinese Medicine with the flow of Reiki energy. Whether you're working with others or walking your own healing path, I hope these teachings help you remember:

- You are connected.
- You are supported.
- You are part of something greater — and so is your healing.

Trust the rhythm.
Let the energy guide you.
And may you move through life with balance, grace, and wisdom.

With love and elemental light,
Dr. Constance Santego
Grand Reiki Master / Elemental Healing Educator

Just for today, I will let go of worry and trust the flow of life.

About The Author

Dream BIGGER!

Dr. Constance Santego is a Grand Reiki Master, educator, and visionary in the field of holistic health and energy medicine. With over two decades of hands-on experience, she has guided thousands of students and clients through powerful healing transformations rooted in the ancient wisdom of Reiki and the natural rhythms of the body.

Holding both a Ph.D. and a Doctorate in Natural Medicine, Dr. Santego bridges the worlds of science and spirituality with grace. Her work blends modern understanding with time-honored healing traditions—creating a uniquely integrative approach that addresses the body, mind, and spirit as one dynamic system.

Dr. Santego is the founder of the *Reiki Wisdom* series, where she explores innovative and intuitive applications of Reiki energy—expanding beyond traditional hand placements into deeper realms of emotional release, spiritual alignment, and elemental healing. Her books are known for being both accessible and profound, offering practical techniques while honoring the sacred essence of the healing path.

In this volume, *Reiki and the Five Elements*, she invites readers to explore the energetic relationship between the body and nature through the lens of Traditional Chinese Medicine. By aligning Reiki practice with the Five Elements—Water, Wood, Fire, Earth, and Metal—she reveals how practitioners can work in harmony with the seasons, the emotions, and the body's energetic terrain to restore balance and promote transformation.

Throughout her career, Dr. Santego has remained dedicated to one core belief:

True healing begins when we align with nature, trust our inner wisdom, and open to the flow of energy that moves through all things.

Just for today, I will let go of worry and trust the flow of life.

Her teachings empower readers and students to listen deeply, heal intuitively, and live with greater freedom, vitality, and purpose.

Dr. Santego continues to teach, write, and develop programs that inspire holistic practitioners, spiritual seekers, and those committed to walking a healing path—one aligned with the elements, grounded in energy, and infused with soul.

ALSO AVAILABLE

Play the game *Ikona* – Discover Your Inner Genie

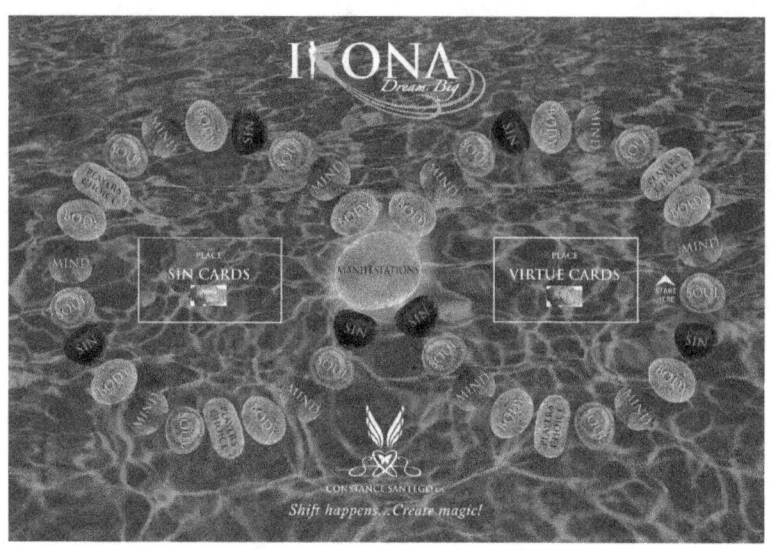

For additional information on

Constance Santego's

wide range of Motivational Products, Coaching Sessions,
Spiritual Retreats,
Live Events and Educational Programs

Go to

www.ConstanceSantego.ca

Follow on Instagram – Constance_Santego and
Facebook – constancesantegoo

Subscribe and receive Free Information and Meditations on
my
YouTube Channel – Constance Santego

Just for today, I will let go of worry and trust the flow of life.

Just for today, I will let go of worry and trust the flow of life.

Just for today, I will let go of worry and trust the flow of life.